Discourse on Inequality

Jean Jacques Rousseau

Table of Contents

Discourse on Inequality..1

    Jean Jacques Rousseau...1

    DEDICATION TO THE REPUBLIC OF GENEVA...1

    PREFACE...10

    A DISSERTATION ON THE ORIGIN AND FOUNDATION OF THE

     INEQUALITY OF MANKIND..15

    THE FIRST PART...17

    THE SECOND PART..41

Discourse on Inequality

Jean Jacques Rousseau

Translated by G. D. H. Cole

A DISCOURSE

ON A SUBJECT PROPOSED BY THE ACADEMY OF DIJON:

WHAT IS THE ORIGIN OF INEQUALITY AMONG MEN,
AND IS IT AUTHORISED BY NATURAL LAW?

We should consider what is natural not in things
depraved but in those which are rightly ordered
according to nature. Aristotle, Politics, Bk. i, ch. 5

DEDICATION TO THE REPUBLIC OF GENEVA

MOST HONOURABLE, MAGNIFICENT AND SOVEREIGN LORDS, convinced that only a virtuous citizen can confer on his country honours which it can accept, I have been for thirty years past working to make myself worthy to offer you some public homage; and, this fortunate opportunity supplementing in some degree the insufficiency of my efforts, I have thought myself entitled to follow in embracing it the dictates of the zeal which inspires me, rather than the right which should have been my authorisation. Having had the happiness to be born among you, how could I reflect on the equality which nature has ordained between men, and the inequality which they have introduced, without reflecting on the profound wisdom by which both are in this State happily combined and made to coincide, in the manner that is most in conformity with natural law, and most favourable to society, to the maintenance of public order and to the happiness of individuals? In my researches after the best rules common sense can lay down for the constitution of a government, I have been so struck at finding them all in actuality in your own, that even had I not been born within your walls I should have thought it indispensable for me to offer this picture of human society to that people, which of all others seems to be possessed of its greatest advantages, and to have best guarded against its abuses.

If I had had to make choice of the place of my birth, I should have preferred a society which had an extent proportionate to the limits of the human faculties; that is, to the possibility of being well governed: in which every person being equal to his occupation, no one should be obliged to commit to others the functions with which he was entrusted: a State, in which all the individuals being well known to one another, neither the secret machinations of vice, nor the modesty of virtue should be able to escape the notice and judgment of the public; and in which the pleasant custom of seeing and knowing one another should make the love of country rather a love of the citizens than of its soil.

I should have wished to be born in a country in which the interest of the Sovereign and that of the people must be single and identical; to the end that all the movements of the machine might tend always to the general happiness. And as this could not be the case, unless the Sovereign and the people were one and the same person, it follows that I should have wished to be born under a democratic government, wisely tempered.

I should have wished to live and die free: that is, so far subject to the laws that neither I, nor anybody else, should be able to cast off their honourable yoke: the easy and salutary yoke which the haughtiest necks bear with the greater docility, as they are made to bear no other.

I should have wished then that no one within the State should be able to say he was above the law; and that no one without should be able to dictate so that the State should be obliged to recognise his authority. For, be the constitution of a government what it may, if there be within its jurisdiction a single man who is not subject to the law, all the rest are necessarily at his discretion. And if there be a national ruler within, and a foreign ruler without, however they may divide their authority, it is impossible that both should be duly obeyed, or that the State should be well governed.

I should not have chosen to live in a republic of recent institution, however excellent its laws; for fear the government, being perhaps otherwise framed than the circumstances of the moment might require, might disagree with the new citizens, or they with it, and the State run the risk of overthrow and destruction almost as soon as it came into being. For it is with liberty as it is with those solid and succulent foods, or with those generous wines which are well adapted to nourish and fortify robust constitutions that are used to them, but ruin and intoxicate weak and delicate constitutions to which they are not suited. Peoples once accustomed to masters are not in a condition to do without them. If they attempt to shake off the yoke, they still more estrange themselves from freedom, as, by mistaking for it an unbridled license to which it is diametrically opposed, they nearly always manage, by their revolutions, to hand themselves over to seducers, who only make their chains heavier than before. The Roman people itself, a model for all free peoples, was wholly incapable of governing itself when it escaped from the oppression of the Tarquins. Debased by slavery, and the ignominious tasks which had been imposed upon it, it was at first no better than a stupid mob, which it was necessary to control and govern with the greatest wisdom; in order that, being accustomed by degrees to breathe the health–giving air of liberty, minds which had been enervated or rather brutalised under tyranny, might gradually acquire that severity of morals and spirit of fortitude which made it at length the people of all most worthy of respect. I should, then, have sought out for my country some peaceful and happy Republic, of an antiquity that lost itself, as it were, in the night of time: which had experienced only such shocks as served to manifest and strengthen the courage and patriotism of its subjects; and whose citizens, long accustomed to a wise independence, were not only free, but worthy to be so.

I should have wished to choose myself a country, diverted, by a fortunate impotence, from the brutal love of conquest, and secured, by a still more fortunate situation, from the fear of becoming itself the conquest of other States: a free city situated between several nations, none of which should have any interest in attacking it, while each had an interest in preventing it from being attacked by the others; in short, a Republic which should have nothing to tempt the ambition of its neighbours, but might reasonably depend on their assistance in case of need. It follows that a republican State so happily situated could have nothing to fear but from itself; and that, if its members trained themselves to the use of arms, it would be rather to keep alive that military ardour and courageous spirit which are so proper among freemen, and tend to keep up their taste for liberty, than from the necessity of providing for their defence.

I should have sought a country, in which the right of legislation was vested in all the citizens; for who can judge better than they of the conditions under which they had best dwell together in the same society? Not that I should have approved of Plebiscita, like those among the Romans; in which the rulers in the State, and those most interested in its preservation, were excluded from the deliberations on which in many cases its security depended; and in which, by the most absurd inconsistency, the magistrates were deprived of rights which the meanest citizens enjoyed.

On the contrary, I should have desired that, in order to prevent self–interested and ill–conceived projects, and all such dangerous innovations as finally ruined the Athenians, each man should not be at liberty to propose new laws at pleasure; but that this right should belong exclusively to the magistrates; and that even they should use it with so much caution, the people, on its side, be so reserved in giving its consent to such laws, and the promulgation of them be attended with so much solemnity, that before the constitution could be upset by them, there might be time enough for all to be convinced, that it is above all the great antiquity of the laws which makes them sacred and venerable, that men soon learn to despise laws which they see daily altered, and that States, by accustoming themselves to neglect their ancient customs under the pretext of improvement, often introduce greater evils than those they endeavour to remove.

I should have particularly avoided, as necessarily ill–governed, a Republic in which the people, imagining themselves in a position to do without magistrates, or at least to leave them with only a precarious authority, should imprudently have kept for themselves the administration of civil affairs and the execution of their own laws. Such must have been the rude constitution of primitive governments, directly emerging from a state of nature; and this was another of the vices that contributed to the downfall of the Republic of Athens.

But I should have chosen a community in which the individuals, content with sanctioning their laws, and deciding the most important public affairs in general assembly and on the motion of the rulers, had established honoured tribunals, carefully distinguished the several departments, and elected year by year some of the most capable and upright of their fellow–citizens to administer justice and govern the State; a community, in short, in which the virtue of the magistrates thus bearing witness to the wisdom of the people, each class reciprocally did the other honour. If in such a case any fatal misunderstandings arose to disturb the public peace, even these intervals of blindness and error would bear the marks of moderation, mutual esteem, and a common respect for the laws; which are sure signs and pledges of a reconciliation as lasting as sincere. Such are the advantages, most honourable, magnificent and sovereign lords, which I should have sought in the country in which I should have chosen to be born. And if providence had added to all these a delightful situation, a temperate climate, a fertile soil, and the most beautiful countryside under Heaven, I should have desired only, to complete my felicity, the peaceful enjoyment of all these blessings, in the bosom of this happy country; to live at peace in the sweet society of my fellow–citizens, and practising towards them, from their own example, the duties of friendship, humanity, and every other virtue, to leave behind me the honourable memory of a good man, and an upright and virtuous patriot.

But, if less fortunate or too late grown wise, I had seen myself reduced to end an infirm and languishing life in other climates, vainly regretting that peaceful repose which I had forfeited in the imprudence of youth, I should at least have entertained the same feelings in my heart, though denied the opportunity of making use of them in my native country. Filled with a tender and disinterested love for my distant fellow–citizens, I should have addressed them from my heart, much in the following terms.

"My dear fellow–citizens, or rather my brothers, since the ties of blood, as well as the laws, unite almost all of us, it gives me pleasure that I cannot think of you, without thinking, at the same time, of all the blessings you enjoy, and of which none of you, perhaps, more deeply feels the value than I who have lost them. The more I reflect on your civil and political condition, the less can I conceive that the nature of human affairs could admit of a better. In all other governments, when there is a question of ensuring the greatest good of the State, nothing gets beyond projects and ideas, or at best bare possibilities. But as for you, your happiness is complete, and you have nothing to do but enjoy it; you require nothing more to be made perfectly happy, than to know how to be satisfied with being so. Your sovereignty, acquired or recovered by the sword, and maintained for two centuries past by your valour and wisdom, is at length fully and universally acknowledged. Your boundaries are fixed, your rights confirmed and your repose secured by honourable treaties. Your constitution is excellent, being not only dictated by the profoundest wisdom, but guaranteed by great and friendly powers. Your State enjoys perfect tranquillity; you have neither wars nor conquerors to fear; you have no other master than the wise laws you have yourselves made; and these are administered by upright magistrates of your own choosing. You are neither so wealthy as to be enervated by effeminacy, and thence to lose, in the pursuit of frivolous pleasures, the taste for real happiness and solid virtue; nor poor enough to require more assistance from abroad than your own industry is sufficient to procure you. In the meantime the precious privilege of liberty, which in great nations is maintained only by submission to the most exorbitant impositions, costs you hardly anything for its preservation.

May a Republic, so wisely and happily constituted, last for ever, for an example to other nations, and for the felicity of its own citizens! This is the only prayer you have left to make, the only precaution that remains to be taken. It depends, for the future, on yourselves alone (not to make you happy, for your ancestors have saved you that trouble), but to render that happiness lasting, by your wisdom in its enjoyment. It is on your constant union, your obedience to the laws, and your respect for their ministers, that your preservation depends. If there remains among you the smallest trace of bitterness or distrust, hasten to destroy it, as an accursed leaven which sooner or later must bring misfortune and ruin on the State. I conjure you all to look into your hearts, and to hearken to the secret voice of conscience. Is there any among you who can find, throughout the universe, a more upright, more enlightened and more honourable body than your magistracy? Do not all its members set you an example of moderation, of simplicity of manners, of respect for the laws, and of the most sincere harmony? Place, therefore, without reserve, in such wise superiors, that salutary confidence which reason ever owes to virtue. Consider that they are your own choice, that they justify that choice, and that the honours due to those whom you have dignified are necessarily yours by reflexion. Not one of you is so ignorant as not to know that, when the laws lose their force and those who defend them their authority, security and liberty are universally impossible. Why, therefore, should you hesitate to do that cheerfully and with just confidence which you would all along have been bound to do by your true interest, your duty and reason itself?

Let not a culpable and pernicious indifference to the maintenance of the constitution ever induce you to neglect, in case of need, the prudent advice of the most enlightened and zealous of your fellow–citizens; but let equity, moderation and firmness of resolution continue to regulate all your proceedings, and to exhibit you to the whole universe as the example of a valiant and modest people, jealous equally of their honour and of their liberty. Beware particularly, as the last piece of advice I shall give you, of sinister constructions and venomous rumours, the secret motives of which are often more dangerous than the actions at which they are levelled. A whole house will be awake and take the first alarm given by a good and trusty watch–dog, who barks only at the approach of thieves; but we hate the importunity of those noisy curs, which are perpetually disturbing the public repose, and whose continual ill–timed warnings prevent our attending to them, when they may perhaps be necessary."

And you, most honourable and magnificent lords, the worthy and revered magistrates of a free people, permit me to offer you in particular my duty and homage. If there is in the world a station capable of conferring honour on those who fill it, it is undoubtedly that which virtue and talents combine to bestow, that of which you have made yourselves worthy, and to which you have been promoted by your fellow-citizens. Their worth adds a new lustre to your own; while, as you have been chosen, by men capable of governing others, to govern themselves, I cannot but hold you as much superior to all other magistrates, as a free people, and particularly that over which you have the honour to preside, is by its wisdom and its reason superior to the populace of other States.

Be it permitted me to cite an example of which there ought to have existed better records, and one which will be ever near to my heart. I cannot recall to mind, without the sweetest emotions, the memory of that virtuous citizen, to whom I owe my being, and by whom I was often instructed, in my infancy, in the respect which is due to you. I see him still, living by the work of his hands, and feeding his soul on the sublimest truths. I see the works of Tacitus, Plutarch, and Grotius lying before him in the midst of the tools of his trade. At his side stands his dear son, receiving, alas with too little profit, the tender instructions of the best of fathers. But, if the follies of youth made me for a while forget his wise lessons, I have at length the happiness to be conscious that, whatever propensity one may have to vice, it is not easy for an education, with which love has mingled, to be entirely thrown away.

Such, my most honourable and magnificent lords, are the citizens, and even the common inhabitants of the State which you govern; such are those intelligent and sensible men, of whom, under the name of workmen and the people, it is usual, in other nations, to have a low and false opinion. My father, I own with pleasure, was in no way distinguished among his fellow-citizens. He was only such as they all are; and yet, such as he was, there is no country, in which his acquaintance would not have been coveted, and cultivated even with advantage by men of the highest character. It would not become me, nor is it, thank Heaven, at all necessary for me to remind you of the regard which such men have a right to expect of their magistrates, to whom they are equal both by education and by the rights of nature and birth, and inferior only, by their own will, by that preference which they owe to your merit, and, for giving you, can claim some sort of acknowledgment on your side. It is with a lively satisfaction I understand that the greatest candour and condescension attend, in all your behaviour towards them, on that gravity which becomes the ministers of the law; and that you so well repay them, by your esteem and attention, the respect and obedience which they owe to you. This conduct is not only just but prudent; as it happily tends to obliterate the memory of many unhappy events, which ought to be buried in eternal oblivion. It is also so much the more judicious, as it tends to make this generous and equitable people find a pleasure in their duty; to make them naturally love to do you honour, and to cause those who are the most zealous in the maintenance of their own rights to be at the same time the most disposed to respect yours.

It ought not to be thought surprising that the rulers of a civil society should have the welfare and glory of their communities at heart: but it is uncommonly fortunate for the peace of men, when those persons who look upon themselves as the magistrates, or rather the masters of a more holy and sublime country, show some love for the earthly country which maintains them. I am happy in having it in my power to make so singular an exception in our favour, and to be able to rank, among its best citizens, those zealous depositaries of the sacred articles of faith established by the laws, those venerable shepherds of souls whose powerful and captivating eloquence are so much the better calculated to bear to men's hearts the maxims of the gospel, as they are themselves the first to put them into practice. All the world knows of the great success with which the art of the pulpit is cultivated at Geneva; but men are so used to hearing divines preach one thing and practise another, that few have a chance of knowing how far the spirit of Christianity, holiness of manners, severity towards themselves and indulgence towards their neighbours, prevail throughout the whole body of our ministers. It is, perhaps, given to the city of Geneva alone, to produce the edifying example of so perfect a union between its clergy and men of letters. It is in great measure on their wisdom, their known moderation, and their zeal for the prosperity of the State that I build my hopes of its perpetual tranquillity. At the same time, I notice, with a pleasure mingled with surprise and veneration, how much they detest the frightful maxims of those accursed and barbarous men, of whom history furnishes us with more than one example; who, in order to support the pretended rights of God, that is to say their own interests, have been so much the less greedy of human blood, as they were more hopeful their own in particular would be always respected.

I must not forget that precious half of the Republic, which makes the happiness of the other; and whose sweetness and prudence preserve its tranquillity and virtue. Amiable and virtuous daughters of Geneva, it will be always the lot of your sex to govern ours.

8

Happy are we, so long as your chaste influence, solely exercised within the limits of conjugal union, is exerted only for the glory of the State and the happiness of the public. It was thus the female sex commanded at Sparta; and thus you deserve to command at Geneva. What man can be such a barbarian as to resist the voice of honour and reason, coming from the lips of an affectionate wife? Who would not despise the vanities of luxury, on beholding the simple and modest attire which, from the lustre it derives from you, seems the most favourable to beauty? It is your task to perpetuate, by your insinuating influence and your innocent and amiable rule, a respect for the laws of the State, and harmony among the citizens. It is yours to reunite divided families by happy marriages; and, above all things, to correct, by the persuasive sweetness of your lessons and the modest graces of your conversation, those extravagancies which our young people pick up in other countries, whence, instead of many useful things by which they might profit, they bring home hardly anything, besides a puerile air and a ridiculous manner, acquired among loose women, but an admiration for I know not what so-called grandeur, and paltry recompenses for being slaves, which can never come near the real greatness of liberty. Continue, therefore, always to be what you are, the chaste guardians of our morals, and the sweet security for our peace, exerting on every occasion the privileges of the heart and of nature, in the interests of duty and virtue.

I flatter myself that I shall never be proved to have been mistaken, in building on such a foundation my hopes of the general happiness of the citizens and the glory of the Republic. It must be confessed, however, that with all these advantages, it will not shine with that lustre, by which the eyes of most men are dazzled; a puerile and fatal taste for which is the most mortal enemy of happiness and liberty.

Let our dissolute youth seek elsewhere light pleasures and long repentances. Let our pretenders to taste admire elsewhere the grandeur of palaces, the beauty of equipages, sumptuous furniture, the pomp of public entertainments, and all the refinements of luxury and effeminacy. Geneva boasts nothing but men; such a sight has nevertheless a value of its own, and those who have a taste for it are well worth the admirers of all the rest.

Deign, most honourable, magnificent and sovereign lords, to receive, and with equal goodness, this respectful testimony of the interest I take in your common prosperity. And, if I have been so unhappy as to be guilty of any indiscreet transport in this glowing effusion of my heart, I beseech you to pardon me, and to attribute it to the tender affection of a true patriot, and to the ardent and legitimate zeal of a man, who can imagine for himself no greater felicity than to see you happy.

Most honourable, magnificent and sovereign lords, I am, with the most profound respect,

Your most humble and obedient servant and fellow–citizen.

J. J. ROUSSEAU

Chambéry, June 12, 1754

PREFACE

OF all human sciences the most useful and most imperfect appears to me to be that of mankind: and I will venture to say, the single inscription on the Temple of Delphi contained a precept more difficult and more important than is to be found in all the huge volumes that moralists have ever written. I consider the subject of the following discourse as one of the most interesting questions philosophy can propose, and unhappily for us, one of the most thorny that philosophers can have to solve. For how shall we know the source of inequality between men, if we do not begin by knowing mankind? And how shall man hope to see himself as nature made him, across all the changes which the succession of place and time must have produced in his original constitution? How can he distinguish what is fundamental in his nature from the changes and additions which his circumstances and the advances he has made have introduced to modify his primitive condition? Like the statue of Glaucus, which was so disfigured by time, seas and tempests, that it looked more like a wild beast than a god, the human soul, altered in society by a thousand causes perpetually recurring, by the acquisition of a multitude of truths and errors, by the changes happening to the constitution of the body, and by the continual jarring of the passions, has, so to speak, changed in appearance, so as to be hardly recognisable. Instead of a being, acting constantly from fixed and invariable principles, instead of that celestial and majestic simplicity, impressed on it by its divine Author, we find in it only the frightful contrast of passion mistaking itself for reason, and of understanding grown delirious.

It is still more cruel that, as every advance made by the human species removes it still farther from its primitive state, the more discoveries we make, the more we deprive ourselves of the means of making the most important of all. Thus it is, in one sense, by our very study of man, that the knowledge of him is put out of our power.

It is easy to perceive that it is in these successive changes in the constitution of man that we must look for the origin of those differences which now distinguish men, who, it is allowed, are as equal among themselves as were the animals of every kind, before physical causes had introduced those varieties which are now observable among some of them.

It is, in fact, not to be conceived that these primary changes, however they may have arisen, could have altered, all at once and in the same manner, every individual of the species. It is natural to think that, while the condition of some of them grew better or worse, and they were acquiring various good or bad qualities not inherent in their nature, there were others who continued a longer time in their original condition. Such was doubtless the first source of the inequality of mankind, which it is much easier to point out thus in general terms, than to assign with precision to its actual causes.

Let not my readers therefore imagine that I flatter myself with having seen what it appears to me so difficult to discover. I have here entered upon certain arguments, and risked some conjectures, less in the hope of solving the difficulty, than with a view to throwing some light upon it, and reducing the question to its proper form. Others may easily proceed farther on the same road, and yet no one find it very easy to get to the end. For it is by no means a light undertaking to distinguish properly between what is original and what is artificial in the actual nature of man, or to form a true idea of a state which no longer exists, perhaps never did exist, and probably never will exist; and of which, it is, nevertheless, necessary to have true ideas, in order to form a proper judgment of our present state. It requires, indeed, more philosophy than can be imagined to enable any one to determine exactly what precautions he ought to take, in order to make solid observations on this subject; and it appears to me that a good solution of the following problem would be not unworthy of the Aristotles and Plinys of the present age. What experiments would have to be made, to discover the natural man? And how are those experiments to be made in a state of society?

So far am I from undertaking to solve this problem, that I think I have sufficiently considered the subject, to venture to declare beforehand that our greatest philosophers would not be too good to direct such experiments, and our most powerful sovereigns to make them. Such a combination we have very little reason to expect, especially attended with the perseverance, or rather succession of intelligence and goodwill necessary on both sides to success.

These investigations, which are so difficult to make, and have been hitherto so little thought of, are, nevertheless, the only means that remain of obviating a multitude of difficulties which deprive us of the knowledge of the real foundations of human society. It is this ignorance of the nature of man, which casts so much uncertainty and obscurity on the true definition of natural right: for, the idea of right, says Burlamaqui, and more particularly that of natural right, are ideas manifestly relative to the nature of man. It is then from this very nature itself, he goes on, from the constitution and state of man, that we must deduce the first principles of this science.

We cannot see without surprise and disgust how little agreement there is between the different authors who have treated this great subject. Among the more important writers there are scarcely two of the same mind about it. Not to speak of the ancient philosophers, who seem to have done their best purposely to contradict one another on the most fundamental principles, the Roman jurists subjected man and the other animals indiscriminately to the same natural law, because they considered, under that name, rather the law which nature imposes on herself than that which she prescribes to others; or rather because of the particular acceptation of the term law among those jurists; who seem on this occasion to have understood nothing more by it than the general relations established by nature between all animated beings, for their common preservation. The moderns, understanding, by the term law, merely a rule prescribed to a moral being, that is to say intelligent, free and considered in his relations to other beings, consequently confine the jurisdiction of natural law to man, as the only animal endowed with reason. But, defining this law, each after his own fashion, they have established it on such metaphysical principles, that there are very few persons among us capable of comprehending them, much less of discovering them for themselves. So that the definitions of these learned men, all differing in everything else, agree only in this, that it is impossible to comprehend the law of nature, and consequently to obey it, without being a very subtle casuist and a profound metaphysician. All which is as much as to say that mankind must have employed, in the establishment of society, a capacity which is acquired only with great difficulty, and by very few persons, even in a state of society.

Discourse on Inequality

Knowing so little of nature, and agreeing so ill about the meaning of the word law, it would be difficult for us to fix on a good definition of natural law. Thus all the definitions we meet with in books, setting aside their defect in point of uniformity, have yet another fault, in that they are derived from many kinds of knowledge, which men do not possess naturally, and from advantages of which they can have no idea until they have already departed from that state. Modern writers begin by inquiring what rules it would be expedient for men to agree on for their common interest, and then give the name of natural law to a collection of these rules, without any other proof than the good that would result from their being universally practised. This is undoubtedly a simple way of making definitions, and of explaining the nature of things by almost arbitrary conveniences.

But as long as we are ignorant of the natural man, it is in vain for us to attempt to determine either the law originally prescribed to him, or that which is best adapted to his constitution. All we can know with any certainty respecting this law is that, if it is to be a law, not only the wills of those it obliges must be sensible of their submission to it; but also, to be natural, it must come directly from the voice of nature.

Throwing aside, therefore, all those scientific books, which teach us only to see men such as they have made themselves, and contemplating the first and most simple operations of the human soul, I think I can perceive in it two principles prior to reason, one of them deeply interesting us in our own welfare and preservation, and the other exciting a natural repugnance at seeing any other sensible being, and particularly any of our own species, suffer pain or death. It is from the agreement and combination which the understanding is in a position to establish between these two principles, without its being necessary to introduce that of sociability, that all the rules of natural right appear to me to be derived — rules which our reason is afterwards obliged to establish on other foundations, when by its successive developments it has been led to suppress nature itself.

In proceeding thus, we shall not be obliged to make man a philosopher before he is a man. His duties toward others are not dictated to him only by the later lessons of wisdom; and, so long as he does not resist the internal impulse of compassion, he will never hurt any other man, nor even any sentient being, except on those lawful occasions on which his own preservation is concerned and he is obliged to give himself the preference. By this method also we put an end to the time-honoured disputes concerning the participation of animals in natural law: for it is clear that, being destitute of intelligence and liberty, they cannot recognise that law; as they partake, however, in some measure of our nature, in consequence of the sensibility with which they are endowed, they ought to partake of natural right; so that mankind is subjected to a kind of obligation even toward the brutes. It appears, in fact, that if I am bound to do no injury to my fellow–creatures, this is less because they are rational than because they are sentient beings: and this quality, being common both to men and beasts, ought to entitle the latter at least to the privilege of not being wantonly ill–treated by the former.

The very study of the original man, of his real wants, and the fundamental principles of his duty, is besides the only proper method we can adopt to obviate all the difficulties which the origin of moral inequality presents, on the true foundations of the body politic, on the reciprocal rights of its members, and on many other similar topics equally important and obscure.

If we look at human society with a calm and disinterested eye, it seems, at first, to show us only the violence of the powerful and the oppression of the weak. The mind is shocked at the cruelty of the one, or is induced to lament the blindness of the other; and as nothing is less permanent in life than those external relations, which are more frequently produced by accident than wisdom, and which are called weakness or power, riches or poverty, all human institutions seem at first glance to be founded merely on banks of shifting sand. It is only by taking a closer look, and removing the dust and sand that surround the edifice, that we perceive the immovable basis on which it is raised, and learn to respect its foundations. Now, without a serious study of man, his natural faculties and their successive development, we shall never be able to make these necessary distinctions, or to separate, in the actual constitution of things, that which is the effect of the divine will, from the innovations attempted by human art. The political and moral investigations, therefore, to which the important question before us leads, are in every respect useful; while the hypothetical history of governments affords a lesson equally instructive to mankind.

In considering what we should have become, had we been left to ourselves, we should learn to bless Him, whose gracious hand, correcting our institutions, and giving them an immovable basis, has prevented those disorders which would otherwise have arisen from them, and caused our happiness to come from those very sources which seemed likely to involve us in misery.

A DISSERTATION ON THE ORIGIN AND FOUNDATION OF THE INEQUALITY OF MANKIND

IT is of man that I have to speak; and the question I am investigating shows me that it is to men that I must address myself: for questions of this sort are not asked by those who are afraid to honour truth. I shall then confidently uphold the cause of humanity before the wise men who invite me to do so, and shall not be dissatisfied if I acquit myself in a manner worthy of my subject and of my judges.

I conceive that there are two kinds of inequality among the human species; one, which I call natural or physical, because it is established by nature, and consists in a difference of age, health, bodily strength, and the qualities of the mind or of the soul: and another, which may be called moral or political inequality, because it depends on a kind of convention, and is established, or at least authorised by the consent of men. This latter consists of the different privileges, which some men enjoy to the prejudice of others; such as that of being more rich, more honoured, more powerful or even in a position to exact obedience.

It is useless to ask what is the source of natural inequality, because that question is answered by the simple definition of the word. Again, it is still more useless to inquire whether there is any essential connection between the two inequalities; for this would be only asking, in other words, whether those who command are necessarily better than those who obey, and if strength of body or of mind, wisdom or virtue are always found in particular individuals, in proportion to their power or wealth: a question fit perhaps to be discussed by slaves in the hearing of their masters, but highly unbecoming to reasonable and free men in search of the truth.

The subject of the present discourse, therefore, is more precisely this. To mark, in the progress of things, the moment at which right took the place of violence and nature became subject to law, and to explain by what sequence of miracles the strong came to submit to serve the weak, and the people to purchase imaginary repose at the expense of real felicity.

The philosophers, who have inquired into the foundations of society, have all felt the necessity of going back to a state of nature; but not one of them has got there. Some of them have not hesitated to ascribe to man, in such a state, the idea of just and unjust, without troubling themselves to show that he must be possessed of such an idea, or that it could be of any use to him. Others have spoken of the natural right of every man to keep what belongs to him, without explaining what they meant by belongs. Others again, beginning by giving the strong authority over the weak, proceeded directly to the birth of government, without regard to the time that must have elapsed before the meaning of the words authority and government could have existed among men. Every one of them, in short, constantly dwelling on wants, avidity, oppression, desires and pride, has transferred to the state of nature ideas which were acquired in society; so that, in speaking of the savage, they described the social man. It has not even entered into the heads of most of our writers to doubt whether the state of nature ever existed; but it is clear from the Holy Scriptures that the first man, having received his understanding and commandments immediately from God, was not himself in such a state; and that, if we give such credit to the writings of Moses as every Christian philosopher ought to give, we must deny that, even before the deluge, men were ever in the pure state of nature; unless, indeed, they fell back into it from some very extraordinary circumstance; a paradox which it would be very embarrassing to defend, and quite impossible to prove.

Let us begin then by laying facts aside, as they do not affect the question. The investigations we may enter into, in treating this subject, must not be considered as historical truths, but only as mere conditional and hypothetical reasonings, rather calculated to explain the nature of things, than to ascertain their actual origin; just like the hypotheses which our physicists daily form respecting the formation of the world. Religion commands us to believe that, God Himself having taken men out of a state of nature immediately after the creation, they are unequal only because it is His will they should be so: but it does not forbid us to form conjectures based solely on the nature of man, and the beings around him, concerning what might have become of the human race, if it had been left to itself. This then is the question asked me, and that which I propose to discuss in the following discourse. As my subject interests mankind in general, I shall endeavour to make use of a style adapted to all nations, or rather, forgetting time and place, to attend only to men to whom I am speaking. I shall suppose myself in the Lyceum of Athens, repeating the lessons of my masters, with Plato and Xenocrates for judges, and the whole human race for audience.

O man, of whatever country you are, and whatever your opinions may be, behold your history, such as I have thought to read it, not in books written by your fellow–creatures, who are liars, but in nature, which never lies. All that comes from her will be true; nor will you meet with anything false, unless I have involuntarily put in something of my own. The times of which I am going to speak are very remote: how much are you changed from what you once were! It is, so to speak, the life of your species which I am going to write, after the qualities which you have received, which your education and habits may have depraved, but cannot have entirely destroyed. There is, I feel, an age at which the individual man would wish to stop: you are about to inquire about the age at which you would have liked your whole species to stand still. Discontented with your present state, for reasons which threaten your unfortunate descendants with still greater discontent, you will perhaps wish it were in your power to go back; and this feeling should be a panegyric on your first ancestors, a criticism of your contemporaries, and a terror to the unfortunates who will come after you.

THE FIRST PART

IMPORTANT as it may be, in order to judge rightly of the natural state of man, to consider him from his origin, and to examine him, as it were, in the embryo of his species; I shall not follow his organisation through its successive developments, nor shall I stay to inquire what his animal system must have been at the beginning, in order to become at length what it actually is. I shall not ask whether his long nails were at first, as Aristotle supposes, only crooked talons; whether his whole body, like that of a bear, was not covered with hair; or whether the fact that he walked upon all fours, with his looks directed toward the earth, confined to a horizon of a few paces, did not at once point out the nature and limits of his ideas. On this subject I could form none but vague and almost imaginary conjectures. Comparative anatomy has as yet made too little progress, and the observations of naturalists are too uncertain to afford an adequate basis for any solid reasoning. So that, without having recourse to the supernatural information given us on this head, or paying any regard to the changes which must have taken place in the internal, as well as the external, conformation of man, as he applied his limbs to new uses, and fed himself on new kinds of food, I shall suppose his conformation to have been at all times what it appears to us at this day; that he always walked on two legs, made use of his hands as we do, directed his looks over all nature, and measured with his eyes the vast expanse of Heaven.

If we strip this being, thus constituted, of all the supernatural gifts he may have received, and all the artificial faculties he can have acquired only by a long process; if we consider him, in a word, just as he must have come from the hands of nature, we behold in him an animal weaker than some, and less agile than others; but, taking him all round, the most advantageously organised of any. I see him satisfying his hunger at the first oak, and slaking his thirst at the first brook; finding his bed at the foot of the tree which afforded him a repast; and, with that, all his wants supplied.

While the earth was left to its natural fertility and covered with immense forests, whose trees were never mutilated by the axe, it would present on every side both sustenance and shelter for every species of animal. Men, dispersed up and down among the rest, would observe and imitate their industry, and thus attain even to the instinct of the beasts, with the advantage that, whereas every species of brutes was confined to one particular instinct, man, who perhaps has not any one peculiar to himself, would appropriate them all, and live upon most of those different foods which other animals shared among themselves; and thus would find his subsistence much more easily than any of the rest.

Accustomed from their infancy to the inclemencies of the weather and the rigour of the seasons, inured to fatigue, and forced, naked and unarmed, to defend themselves and their prey from other ferocious animals, or to escape them by flight, men would acquire a robust and almost unalterable constitution. The children, bringing with them into the world the excellent constitution of their parents, and fortifying it by the very exercises which first produced it, would thus acquire all the vigour of which the human frame is capable. Nature in this case treats them exactly as Sparta treated the children of her citizens: those who come well formed into the world she renders strong and robust, and all the rest she destroys; differing in this respect from our modern communities, in which the State, by making children a burden to their parents, kills them indiscriminately before they are born.

The body of a savage man being the only instrument he understands, he uses it for various purposes, of which ours, for want of practice, are incapable: for our industry deprives us of that force and agility, which necessity obliges him to acquire. If he had had an axe, would he have been able with his naked arm to break so large a branch from a tree? If he had had a sling, would he have been able to throw a stone with so great velocity? If he had had a ladder, would he have been so nimble in climbing a tree? If he had had a horse, would he have been himself so swift of foot? Give civilised man time to gather all his machines about him, and he will no doubt easily beat the savage; but if you would see a still more unequal contest, set them together naked and unarmed, and you will soon see the advantage of having all our forces constantly at our disposal, of being always prepared for every event, and of carrying one's self, as it were, perpetually whole and entire about one.

Hobbes contends that man is naturally intrepid, and is intent only upon attacking and fighting. Another illustrious philosopher holds the opposite, and Cumberland and Puffendorf also affirm that nothing is more timid and fearful than man in the state of nature; that he is always in a tremble, and ready to fly at the least noise or the slightest movement. This may be true of things he does not know; and I do not doubt his being terrified by every novelty that presents itself, when he neither knows the physical good or evil he may expect from it, nor can make a comparison between his own strength and the dangers he is about to encounter. Such circumstances, however, rarely occur in a state of nature, in which all things proceed in a uniform manner, and the face of the earth is not subject to those sudden and continual changes which arise from the passions and caprices of bodies of men living together. But savage man, living dispersed among other animals, and finding himself betimes in a situation to measure his strength with theirs, soon comes to compare himself with them; and, perceiving that he surpasses them more in adroitness than they surpass him in strength, learns to be no longer afraid of them. Set a bear, or a wolf, against a robust, agile, and resolute savage, as they all are, armed with stones and a good cudgel, and you will see that the danger will be at least on both sides, and that, after a few trials of this kind, wild beasts, which are not fond of attacking each other, will not be at all ready to attack man, whom they will have found to be as wild and ferocious as themselves. With regard to such animals as have really more strength than man has adroitness, he is in the same situation as all weaker animals, which notwithstanding are still able to subsist; except indeed that he has the advantage that, being equally swift of foot, and finding an almost certain place of refuge in every tree, he is at liberty to take or leave it at every encounter, and thus to fight or fly, as he chooses. Add to this that it does not appear that any animal naturally makes war on man, except in case of self–defence or excessive hunger, or betrays any of those violent antipathies, which seem to indicate that one species is intended by nature for the food of another.

This is doubtless why negroes and savages are so little afraid of the wild beasts they may meet in the woods. The Caraibs of Venezuela among others live in this respect in absolute security and without the smallest inconvenience. Though they are almost naked, Francis Corréal tells us, they expose themselves freely in the woods, armed only with bows and arrows; but no one has ever heard of one of them being devoured by wild beasts.

But man has other enemies more formidable, against which is is not provided with such means of defence: these are the natural infirmities of infancy, old age, and illness of every kind, melancholy proofs of our weakness, of which the two first are common to all animals, and the last belongs chiefly to man in a state of society. With regard to infancy, it is observable that the mother, carrying her child always with her, can nurse it with much greater ease than the females of many other animals, which are forced to be perpetually going and coming, with great fatigue, one way to find subsistence, and another to suckle or feed their young. It is true that if the woman happens to perish, the infant is in great danger of perishing with her; but this risk is common to many other species of animals, whose young take a long time before they are able to provide for themselves. And if our infancy is longer than theirs, our lives are longer in proportion; so that all things are in this respect fairly equal; though there are other rules to be considered regarding the duration of the first period of life, and the number of young, which do not affect the present subject. In old age, when men are less active and perspire little, the need for food diminishes with the ability to provide it. As the savage state also protects them from gout and rheumatism, and old age is, of all ills, that which human aid can least alleviate, they cease to be, without others perceiving that they are no more, and almost without perceiving it themselves.

With respect to sickness, I shall not repeat the vain and false declamations which most healthy people pronounce against medicine; but I shall ask if any solid observations have been made from which it may be justly concluded that, in the countries where the art of medicine is most neglected, the mean duration of man's life is less than in those where it is most cultivated. How indeed can this be the case, if we bring on ourselves more diseases than medicine can furnish remedies? The great inequality in manner of living, the extreme idleness of some, and the excessive labour of others, the easiness of exciting and gratifying our sensual appetites, the too exquisite foods of the wealthy which overheat and fill them with indigestion, and, on the other hand, the unwholesome food of the poor, often, bad as it is, insufficient for their needs, which induces them, when opportunity offers, to eat voraciously and overcharge their stomachs; all these, together with sitting up late, and excesses of every kind, immoderate transports of every passion, fatigue, mental exhaustion, the innumerable pains and anxieties inseparable from every condition of life, by which the mind of man is incessantly tormented; these are too fatal proofs that the greater part of our ills are of our own making, and that we might have avoided them nearly all by adhering to that simple, uniform and solitary manner of life which nature prescribed. If she destined man to be healthy, I venture to declare that a state of reflection is a state contrary to nature, and that a thinking man is a depraved animal. When we think of the good constitution of the savages, at least of those whom we have not ruined with our spirituous liquors, and reflect that they are troubled with hardly any disorders, save wounds and old age, we are tempted to believe that, in following the history of civil society, we shall be telling also that of human sickness. Such, at least, was the opinion of Plato, who inferred from certain remedies prescribed, or approved, by Podalirius and Machaon at the siege of Troy, that several sicknesses which these remedies gave rise to in his time, were not then known to mankind: and Celsus tells us that diet, which is now so necessary, was first invented by Hippocrates.

Being subject therefore to so few causes of sickness, man, in the state of nature, can have no need of remedies, and still less of physicians: nor is the human race in this respect worse off than other animals, and it is easy to learn from hunters whether they meet with many infirm animals in the course of the chase. It is certain they frequently meet with such as carry the marks of having been considerably wounded, with many that have had bones or even limbs broken, yet have been healed without any other surgical assistance than that of time, or any other regimen than that of their ordinary life. At the same time their cures seem not to have been less perfect, for their not having been tortured by incisions, poisoned with drugs, or wasted by fasting. In short, however useful medicine, properly administered, may be among us, it is certain that, if the savage, when he is sick and left to himself, has nothing to hope but from nature, he has, on the other hand, nothing to fear but from his disease; which renders his situation often preferable to our own.

We should beware, therefore, of confounding the savage man with the men we have daily before our eyes. Nature treats all the animals left to her care with a predilection that seems to show how jealous she is of that right. The horse, the cat, the bull, and even the ass are generally of greater stature, and always more robust, and have more vigour, strength and courage, when they run wild in the forests than when bred in the stall. By becoming domesticated, they lose half these advantages; and it seems as if all our care to feed and treat them well serves only to deprave them. It is thus with man also: as he becomes sociable and a slave, he grows weak, timid and servile; his effeminate way of life totally enervates his strength and courage. To this it may be added that there is still a greater difference between savage and civilised man, than between wild and tame beasts: for men and brutes having been treated alike by nature, the several conveniences in which men indulge themselves still more than they do their beasts, are so many additional causes of their deeper degeneracy.

It is not therefore so great a misfortune to these primitive men, nor so great an obstacle to their preservation, that they go naked, have no dwellings and lack all the superfluities which we think so necessary. If their skins are not covered with hair, they have no need of such covering in warm climates; and, in cold countries, they soon learn to appropriate the skins of the beasts they have overcome. If they have but two legs to run with, they have two arms to defend themselves with, and provide for their wants. Their children are slowly and with difficulty taught to walk; but their mothers are able to carry them with ease; an advantage which other animals lack, as the mother, if pursued, is forced either to abandon her young, or to regulate her pace by theirs. Unless, in short, we suppose a singular and fortuitous concurrence of circumstances of which I shall speak later, and which would be unlikely to exist, it is plain in every state of the case, that the man who first made himself clothes or a dwelling was furnishing himself with things not at all necessary; for he had till then done without them, and there is no reason why he should not have been able to put up in manhood with the same kind of life as had been his in infancy.

Solitary, indolent, and perpetually accompanied by danger, the savage cannot but be fond of sleep; his sleep too must be light, like that of the animals, which think but little and may be said to slumber all the time they do not think. Self–preservation being his chief and almost sole concern, he must exercise most those faculties which are most concerned with attack or defence, either for overcoming his prey, or for preventing him from becoming the prey of other animals. On the other hand, those organs which are perfected only by softness and sensuality will remain in a gross and imperfect state, incompatible with any sort of delicacy; so that, his senses being divided on this head, his touch and taste will be extremely coarse, his sight, hearing and smell exceedingly fine and subtle. Such in general is the animal condition, and such, according to the narratives of travellers, is that of most savage nations. It is therefore no matter for surprise that the Hottentots of the Cape of Good Hope distinguish ships at sea, with the naked eye, at as great a distance as the Dutch can do with their telescopes; or that the savages of America should trace the Spaniards, by their smell, as well as the best dogs could have done; or that these barbarous peoples feel no pain in going naked, or that they use large quantities of piemento with their food, and drink the strongest European liquors like water.

Hitherto I have considered merely the physical man; let us now take a view of him on his metaphysical and moral side.

I see nothing in any animal but an ingenious machine, to which nature hath given senses to wind itself up, and to guard itself, to a certain degree, against anything that might tend to disorder or destroy it. I perceive exactly the same things in the human machine, with this difference, that in the operations of the brute, nature is the sole agent, whereas man has some share in his own operations, in his character as a free agent. The one chooses and refuses by instinct, the other from an act of free–will: hence the brute cannot deviate from the rule prescribed to it, even when it would be advantageous for it to do so; and, on the contrary, man frequently deviates from such rules to his own prejudice. Thus a pigeon would be starved to death by the side of a dish of the choicest meats, and a cat on a heap of fruit or grain; though it is certain that either might find nourishment in the foods which it thus rejects with disdain, did it think of trying them. Hence it is that dissolute men run into excesses which bring on fevers and death; because the mind depraves the senses, and the will continues to speak when nature is silent.

Every animal has ideas, since it has senses; it even combines those ideas in a certain degree; and it is only in degree that man differs, in this respect, from the brute. Some philosophers have even maintained that there is a greater difference between one man and another than between some men and some beasts. It is not, therefore, so much the understanding that constitutes the specific difference between the man and the brute, as the human quality of free–agency. Nature lays her commands on every animal, and the brute obeys her voice. Man receives the same impulsion, but at the same time knows himself at liberty to acquiesce or resist: and it is particularly in his consciousness of this liberty that the spirituality of his soul is displayed. For physics may explain, in some measure, the mechanism of the senses and the formation of ideas; but in the power of willing or rather of choosing, and in the feeling of this power, nothing is to be found but acts which are purely spiritual and wholly inexplicable by the laws of mechanism.

However, even if the difficulties attending all these questions should still leave room for difference in this respect between men and brutes, there is another very specific quality which distinguishes them, and which will admit of no dispute. This is the faculty of self–improvement, which, by the help of circumstances, gradually develops all the rest of our faculties, and is inherent in the species as in the individual: whereas a brute is, at the end of a few months, all he will ever be during his whole life, and his species, at the end of a thousand years, exactly what it was the first year of that thousand. Why is man alone liable to grow into a dotard? Is it not because he returns, in this, to his primitive state; and that, while the brute, which has acquired nothing and has therefore nothing to lose, still retains the force of instinct, man, who loses, by age or accident, all that his perfectibility had enabled him to gain, falls by this means lower than the brutes themselves? It would be melancholy, were we forced to admit that this distinctive and almost unlimited faculty is the source of all human misfortunes; that it is this which, in time, draws man out of his original state, in which he would have spent his days insensibly in peace and innocence; that it is this faculty, which, successively producing in different ages his discoveries and his errors, his vices and his virtues, makes him at length a tyrant both over himself and over nature.[1] It would be shocking to be obliged to regard as a benefactor the man who first suggested to the Oroonoko Indians the use of the boards they apply to the temples of their children, which secure to them some part at least of their imbecility and original happiness.

Savage man, left by nature solely to the direction of instinct, or rather indemnified for what he may lack by faculties capable at first of supplying its place, and afterwards of raising him much above it, must accordingly begin with purely animal functions: thus seeing and feeling must be his first condition, which would be common to him and all other animals. To will, and not to will, to desire and to fear, must be the first, and almost the only operations of his soul, till new circumstances occasion new developments of his faculties.

Whatever moralists may hold, the human understanding is greatly indebted to the passions, which, it is universally allowed, are also much indebted to the understanding. It is by the activity of the passions that our reason is improved; for we desire knowledge only because we wish to enjoy; and it is impossible to conceive any reason why a person who has neither fears nor desires should give himself the trouble of reasoning. The passions, again, originate in our wants, and their progress depends on that of our knowledge; for we cannot desire or fear anything, except from the idea we have of it, or from the simple impulse of nature. Now savage man, being destitute of every species of intelligence, can have no passions save those of the latter kind: his desires never go beyond his physical wants. The only goods he recognises in the universe are food, a female, and sleep: the only evils he fears are pain and hunger. I say pain, and not death:

24

for no animal can know what it is to die; the knowledge of death and its terrors being one of the first acquisitions made by man in departing from an animal state.

It would be easy, were it necessary, to support this opinion by facts, and to show that, in all the nations of the world, the progress of the understanding has been exactly proportionate to the wants which the peoples had received from nature, or been subjected to by circumstances, and in consequence to the passions that induced them to provide for those necessities. I might instance the arts, rising up in Egypt and expanding with the inundation of the Nile. I might follow their progress into Greece, where they took root afresh, grew up and lowered to the skies, among the rocks and sands of Attica, without being able to germinate on the fertile banks of the Eurotas: I might observe that in general, the people of the North are more industrious than those of the South, because they cannot get on so well without being so: as if nature wanted to equalise matters by giving their understandings the fertility she had refused to their soil.

But who does not see, without recurring to the uncertain testimony of history, that everything seems to remove from savage man both the temptation and the means of changing his condition? His imagination paints no pictures; his heart makes no demands on him. His few wants are so readily supplied, and he is so far from having the knowledge which is needful to make him want more, that he can have neither foresight nor curiosity. The face of nature becomes indifferent to him as it grows familiar. He sees in it always the same order, the same successions: he has not understanding enough to wonder at the greatest miracles; nor is it in his mind that we can expect to find that philosophy man needs, if he is to know how to notice for once what he sees every day. His soul, which nothing disturbs, is wholly wrapped up in the feeling of its present existence, without any idea of the future, however near at hand; while his projects, as limited as his views, hardly extend to the close of day. Such, even at present, is the extent of the native Caribbean's foresight: he will improvidently sell you his cotton−bed in the morning, and come crying in the evening to buy it again, not having foreseen he would want it again the next night.

The more we reflect on this subject, the greater appears the distance between pure sensation and the most simple knowledge: it is impossible indeed to conceive how a man, by his own powers alone, without the aid of communication and the spur of necessity, could have bridged so great a gap. How many ages may have elapsed before mankind were in a position to behold any other fire than that of the heavens. What a multiplicity of chances must have happened to teach them the commonest uses of that element! How often must they have let it out before they acquired the art of reproducing it? and how often may not such a secret have died with him who had discovered it? What shall we say of agriculture, an art which requires so much labour and foresight, which is so dependent on others that it is plain it could only be practised in a society which had at least begun, and which does not serve so much to draw the means of subsistence from the earth — for these it would produce of itself — but to compel it to produce what is most to our taste? But let us suppose that men had so multiplied that the natural produce of the earth was no longer sufficient for their support; a supposition, by the way, which would prove such a life to be very advantageous for the human race; let us suppose that, without forges or workshops, the instruments of husbandry had dropped from the sky into the hands of savages; that they had overcome their natural aversion to continual labour; that they had learnt so much foresight for their needs; that they had divined how to cultivate the earth, to sow grain and plant trees; that they had discovered the arts of grinding corn, and of setting the grape to ferment — all being things that must have been taught them by the gods, since it is not to be conceived how they could discover them for themselves — yet after all this, what man among them would be so absurd as to take the trouble of cultivating a field, which might be stripped of its crop by the first comer, man or beast, that might take a liking to it; and how should each of them resolve to pass his life in wearisome labour, when, the more necessary to him the reward of his labour might be, the surer he would be of not getting it? In a word, how could such a situation induce men to cultivate the earth, till it was regularly parcelled out among them; that is to say, till the state of nature had been abolished?

Were we to suppose savage man as trained in the art of thinking as philosophers make him; were we, like them, to suppose him a very philosopher capable of investigating the sublimest truths, and of forming, by highly abstract chains of reasoning, maxims of reason and justice, deduced from the love of order in general, or the known will of his Creator; in a word, were we to suppose him as intelligent and enlightened, as he must have been, and is in fact found to have been, dull and stupid, what advantage would accrue to the species, from all such metaphysics, which could not be communicated by one to another, but must end with him who made them? What progress could be made by mankind, while dispersed in the woods among other animals? and how far could men improve or mutually enlighten one another, when, having no fixed habitation, and no need of one another's assistance, the same persons hardly met twice in their lives, and perhaps then, without knowing one another or speaking together?

Discourse on Inequality

Let it be considered how many ideas we owe to the use of speech; how far grammar exercises the understanding and facilitates its operations. Let us reflect on the inconceivable pains and the infinite space of time that the first invention of languages must have cost. To these reflections add what preceded, and then judge how many thousand ages must have elapsed in the successive development in the human mind of those operations of which it is capable.

I shall here take the liberty for a moment, of considering the difficulties of the origin of languages, on which subject I might content myself with a simple repetition of the Abbé Condillac's investigations, as they fully confirm my system, and perhaps even first suggested it. But it is plain, from the manner in which this philosopher solves the difficulties he himself raises, concerning the origin of arbitrary signs, that he assumes what I question, viz., that a kind of society must already have existed among the first inventors of language. While I refer, therefore, to his observations on this head, I think it right to give my own, in order to exhibit the same difficulties in a light adapted to my subject. The first which presents itself is to conceive how language can have become necessary; for as there was no communication among men and no need for any, we can neither conceive the necessity of this invention, nor the possibility of it, if it was not somehow indispensable. I might affirm, with many others, that languages arose in the domestic intercourse between parents and their children. But this expedient would not obviate the difficulty, and would besides involve the blunder made by those who, in reasoning on the state of nature, always import into it ideas gathered in a state of society. Thus they constantly consider families as living together under one roof, and the individuals of each as observing among themselves a union as intimate and permanent as that which exists among us, where so many common interests unite them: whereas, in this primitive state, men had neither houses, nor huts, nor any kind of property whatever; every one lived where he could, seldom for more than a single night; the sexes united without design, as accident, opportunity or inclination brought them together, nor had they any great need of words to communicate their designs to each other; and they parted with the same indifference. The mother gave suck to her children at first for her own sake; and afterwards, when habit had made them dear, for theirs: but as soon as they were strong enough to go in search of their own food, they forsook her of their own accord; and, as they had hardly any other method of not losing one another than that of remaining continually within sight, they soon became quite incapable of recognising one another when they happened to meet again. It is farther to be observed that the child, having all his wants to explain, and of course more to say to his mother than the mother could have

27

to say to him, must have borne the brunt of the task of invention, and the language he used would be of his own device, so that the number of languages would be equal to that of the individuals speaking them, and the variety would be increased by the vagabond and roving life they led, which would not give time for any idiom to become constant. For to say that the mother dictated to her child the words he was to use in asking her for one thing or another, is an explanation of how languages already formed are taught, but by no means explains how languages were originally formed.

We will suppose, however, that this first difficulty is obviated. Let us for a moment then take ourselves as being on this side of the vast space which must lie between a pure state of nature and that in which languages had become necessary, and, admitting their necessity, let us inquire how they could first be established. Here we have a new and worse difficulty to grapple with; for if men need speech to learn to think, they must have stood in much greater need of the art of thinking, to be able to invent that of speaking. And though we might conceive how the articulate sounds of the voice came to be taken as the conventional interpreters of our ideas, it would still remain for us to inquire what could have been the interpreters of this convention for those ideas, which, answering to no sensible objects, could not be indicated either by gesture or voice; so that we can hardly form any tolerable conjectures about the origin of this art of communicating our thoughts and establishing a correspondence between minds: an art so sublime, that far distant as it is from its origin, philosophers still behold it at such an immeasurable distance from perfection, that there is none rash enough to affirm it will ever reach it, even though the revolutions time necessarily produces were suspended in its favour, though prejudice should be banished from our academies or condemned to silence, and those learned societies should devote themselves uninterruptedly for whole ages to this thorny question.

The first language of mankind, the most universal and vivid, in a word the only language man needed, before he had occasion to exert his eloquence to persuade assembled multitudes, was the simple cry of nature. But as this was excited only by a sort of instinct on urgent occasions, to implore assistance in case of danger, or relief in case of suffering, it could be of little use in the ordinary course of life, in which more moderate feelings prevail. When the ideas of men began to expand and multiply, and closer communication took place among them, they strove to invent more numerous signs and a more copious language. They multiplied the inflections of the voice, and added gestures, which are in their own nature more expressive, and depend less for their meaning on a prior

28

determination. Visible and movable objects were therefore expressed by gestures, and audible ones by imitative sounds: but, as hardly anything can be indicated by gestures, except objects actually present or easily described, and visible actions; as they are not universally useful — for darkness or the interposition of a material object destroys their efficacy — and as besides they rather request than secure our attention; men at length bethought themselves of substituting for them the articulate sounds of the voice, which, without bearing the same relation to any particular ideas, are better calculated to express them all, as conventional signs. Such an institution could only be made by common consent, and must have been effected in a manner not very easy for men whose gross organs had not been accustomed to any such exercise. It is also in itself still more difficult to conceive, since such a common agreement must have had motives, and speech seems to have been highly necessary to establish the use of it.

It is reasonable to suppose that the words first made use of by mankind had a much more extensive signification than those used in languages already formed, and that ignorant as they were of the division of discourse into its constituent parts, they at first gave every single word the sense of a whole proposition. When they began to distinguish subject and attribute, and noun and verb, which was itself no common effort of genius, substantives were first only so many proper names; the present infinitive was the only tense of verbs; and the very idea of adjectives must have been developed with great difficulty; for every adjective is an abstract idea, and abstractions are painful and unnatural operations.

Every object at first received a particular name without regard to genus or species, which these primitive originators were not in a position to distinguish; every individual presented itself to their minds in isolation, as they are in the picture of nature. If one oak was called A, another was called B; for the primitive idea of two things is that they are not the same, and it often takes a long time for what they have in common to be seen: so that, the narrower the limits of their knowledge of things, the more copious their dictionary must have been. The difficulty of using such a vocabulary could not be easily removed; for, to arrange beings under common and generic denominations, it became necessary to know their distinguishing properties: the need arose for observation and definition, that is to say, for natural history and metaphysics of a far more developed kind than men can at that time have possessed.

Add to this, that general ideas cannot be introduced into the mind without the assistance of words, nor can the understanding seize them except by means of propositions. This is one of the reasons why animals cannot form such ideas, or ever acquire that capacity for self–improvement which depends on them. When a monkey goes from one nut to another, are we to conceive that he entertains any general idea of that kind of fruit, and compares its archetype with the two individual nuts? Assuredly he does not; but the sight of one of these nuts recalls to his memory the sensations which he received from the other, and his eyes, being modified after a certain manner, give information to the palate of the modification it is about to receive. Every general idea is purely intellectual; if the imagination meddles with it ever so little, the idea immediately becomes particular. If you endeavour to trace in your mind the image of a tree in general, you never attain to your end. In spite of all you can do, you will have to see it as great or little, bare or leafy, light or dark, and were you capable of seeing nothing in it but what is common to all trees, it would no longer be like a tree at all. Purely abstract beings are perceivable in the same manner, or are only conceivable by the help of language. The definition of a triangle alone gives you a true idea of it: the moment you imagine a triangle in your mind, it is some particular triangle and not another, and you cannot avoid giving it sensible lines and a coloured area. We must then make use of propositions and of language in order to form general ideas. For no sooner does the imagination cease to operate than the understanding proceeds only by the help of words. If then the first inventors of speech could give names only to ideas they already had, it follows that the first substantives could be nothing more than proper names.

But when our new grammarians, by means of which I have no conception, began to extend their ideas and generalise their terms, the ignorance of the inventors must have confined this method within very narrow limits; and, as they had at first gone too far in multiplying the names of individuals, from ignorance of their genus and species, they made afterwards too few of these, from not having considered beings in all their specific differences. It would indeed have needed more knowledge and experience than they could have, and more pains and inquiry than they would have bestowed, to carry these distinctions to their proper length. If, even to–day, we are continually discovering new species, which have hitherto escaped observation, let us reflect how many of them must have escaped men who judged things merely from their first appearance! It is superfluous to add that the primitive classes and the most general notions must necessarily have escaped their notice also. How, for instance, could they have understood or thought of the words matter, spirit, substance, mode, figure, motion, when even our philosophers, who have so long been making use of them, have themselves the greatest difficulty in understanding them; and when, the ideas attached to them being purely metaphysical, there are no models of them to be found in nature?

But I stop at this point, and ask my judges to suspend their reading a while, to consider, after the invention of physical substantives, which is the easiest part of language to invent, that there is still a great way to go, before the thoughts of men will have found perfect expression and constant form, such as would answer the purposes of public speaking, and produce their effect on society. I beg of them to consider how much time must have been spent, and how much knowledge needed, to find out numbers, abstract terms, aorists and all the tenses of verbs, particles, syntax, the method of connecting propositions, the forms of reasoning, and all the logic of speech. For myself, I am so aghast at the increasing difficulties which present themselves, and so well convinced of the almost demonstrable impossibility that languages should owe their original institution to merely human means, that I leave, to any one who will undertake it, the discussion of the difficult problem, which was most necessary, the existence of society to the invention of language, or the invention of language to the establishment of society. But be the origin of language and society what they may, it may be at least inferred, from the little care which nature has taken to unite mankind by mutual wants, and to facilitate the use of speech, that she has contributed little to make them sociable, and has put little of her own into all they have done to create such bonds of union. It is in fact impossible to conceive why, in a state of nature, one man should stand more in need of the assistance of another, than a monkey or a wolf of the assistance of another of its kind: or, granting that he did, what motives could induce that other to assist him; or, even then, by what means they could agree about the conditions. I know it is incessantly repeated that man would in such a state have been the most miserable of creatures; and indeed, if it be true, as I think I have proved, that he must have lived many ages, before he could have either desire or an opportunity of emerging from it, this would only be an accusation against nature, and not against the being which she had thus unhappily constituted. But as I understand the word miserable, it either has no meaning at all, or else signifies only a painful privation of something, or a state of suffering either in body or soul. I should be glad to have explained to me, what kind of misery a free being, whose heart is at ease and whose body is in health, can possibly suffer. I would ask also, whether a social or a natural life is most likely to become insupportable to those who enjoy it. We see around us hardly a creature in civil society, who does not lament his existence: we even see many deprive themselves of as much of it as they can, and laws human and divine together can hardly put a stop to the disorder. I ask, if it was ever known that a savage took it into his head, when at liberty, to complain of life or to make away with himself. Let us therefore judge, with

31

less vanity, on which side the real misery is found. On the other hand, nothing could be more unhappy than savage man, dazzled by science, tormented by his passions, and reasoning about a state different from his own. It appears that Providence most wisely determined that the faculties, which he potentially possessed, should develop themselves only as occasion offered to exercise them, in order that they might not be superfluous or perplexing to him, by appearing before their time, nor slow and useless when the need for them arose. In instinct alone, he had all he required for living in the state of nature; and with a developed understanding he has only just enough to support life in society.

It appears, at first view, that men in a state of nature, having no moral relations or determinate obligations one with another, could not be either good or bad, virtuous or vicious; unless we take these terms in a physical sense, and call, in an individual, those qualities vices which may be injurious to his preservation, and those virtues which contribute to it; in which case, he would have to be accounted most virtuous, who put least check on the pure impulses of nature. But without deviating from the ordinary sense of the words, it will be proper to suspend the judgment we might be led to form on such a state, and be on our guard against our prejudices, till we have weighed the matter in the scales of impartiality, and seen whether virtues or vices preponderate among civilised men; and whether their virtues do them more good than their vices do harm; till we have discovered, whether the progress of the sciences sufficiently indemnifies them for the mischiefs they do one another, in proportion as they are better informed of the good they ought to do; or whether they would not be, on the whole, in a much happier condition if they had nothing to fear or to hope from any one, than as they are, subjected to universal dependence, and obliged to take everything from those who engage to give them nothing in return.

Above all, let us not conclude, with Hobbes, that because man has no idea of goodness, he must be naturally wicked; that he is vicious because he does not know virtue; that he always refuses to do his fellow-creatures services which he does not think they have a right to demand; or that by virtue of the right he truly claims to everything he needs, he foolishly imagines himself the sole proprietor of the whole universe. Hobbes had seen clearly the defects of all the modern definitions of natural right: but the consequences which he deduces from his own show that he understands it in an equally false sense. In reasoning on the principles he lays down, he ought to have said that the state of nature, being that in which the care for our own preservation is the least prejudicial to that of others, was consequently the best calculated to promote peace, and the most suitable for mankind. He does say the exact opposite, in consequence of having improperly admitted, as a part of savage man's care for self–preservation, the gratification of a multitude of passions which are the work of society, and have made laws necessary. A bad man, he says, is a robust child. But it remains to be proved whether man in a state of nature is this robust child: and, should we grant that he is, what would he infer? Why truly, that if this man, when robust and strong, were dependent on others as he is when feeble, there is no extravagance he would not be guilty of; that he would beat his mother when she was too slow in giving him her breast; that he would strangle one of his younger brothers, if he should be troublesome to him, or bite the arm of another, if he put him to any inconvenience. But that man in the state of nature is both strong and dependent involves two contrary suppositions. Man is weak when he is dependent, and is his own master before he comes to be strong. Hobbes did not reflect that the same cause, which prevents a savage from making use of his reason, as our jurists hold, prevents him also from abusing his faculties, as Hobbes himself allows: so that it may be justly said that savages are not bad merely because they do not know what it is to be good: for it is neither the development of the understanding nor the restraint of law that hinders them from doing ill; but the peacefulness of their passions, and their ignorance of vice: tanto plus in illis proficit vitiorum ignoratio, quam in his cognitio virtutis.[2]

There is another principle which has escaped Hobbes; which, having been bestowed on mankind, to moderate, on certain occasions, the impetuosity of egoism, or, before its birth, the desire of self–preservation, tempers the ardour with which he pursues his own welfare, by an innate repugnance at seeing a fellow–creature suffer.[3] I think I need not fear contradiction in holding man to be possessed of the only natural virtue, which could not be denied him by the most violent detractor of human virtue. I am speaking of compassion, which is a disposition suitable to creatures so weak and subject to so many evils as we certainly are: by so much the more universal and useful to mankind, as it comes before any kind of reflection; and at the same time so natural, that the very brutes themselves sometimes give evident proofs of it. Not to mention the tenderness of mothers for their offspring and the perils they encounter to save them from danger, it is well known that horses show a reluctance to trample on living bodies. One animal never passes by the dead body of another of its species: there are even some which give their fellows a sort of burial; while the mournful lowings of the cattle when they enter the slaughter–house show the impressions made on them by the horrible spectacle which meets them. We find, with pleasure, the author of the Fable of the Bees obliged to own that man is a compassionate and sensible being, and laying aside his cold subtlety of style, in the example he gives, to present us with the pathetic description of a man who, from a place of confinement, is compelled to behold a wild beast tear a child from the arms of its mother, grinding its tender limbs with its murderous teeth, and tearing its palpitating entrails with its claws. What horrid agitation must not the eyewitness of such a scene experience, although he would not be personally concerned! What anxiety would he not suffer at not being able to give any assistance to the fainting mother and the dying infant!

Such is the pure emotion of nature, prior to all kinds of reflection! Such is the force of natural compassion, which the greatest depravity of morals has as yet hardly been able to destroy! for we daily find at our theatres men affected, nay shedding tears at the sufferings of a wretch who, were he in the tyrant's place, would probably even add to the torments of his enemies; like the bloodthirsty Sulla, who was so sensitive to ills he had not caused, or that Alexander of Pheros who did not dare to go and see any tragedy acted, for fear of being seen weeping with Andromache and Priam, though he could listen without emotion to the cries of all the citizens who were daily strangled at his command.

Mollissima corda Humano generi dare se natura fatetur, Quæ lacrimas dedit. Juvenal, Satires, xv. 151[4]

Mandeville well knew that, in spite of all their morality, men would have never been better than monsters, had not nature bestowed on them a sense of compassion, to aid their reason: but he did not see that from this quality alone flow all those social virtues, of which he denied man the possession. But what is generosity, clemency or humanity but compassion applied to the weak, to the guilty, or to mankind in general? Even benevolence and friendship are, if we judge rightly, only the effects of compassion, constantly set upon a particular object: for how is it different to wish that another person may not suffer pain and uneasiness and to wish him happy? Were it even true that pity is no more than a feeling, which puts us in the place of the sufferer, a feeling, obscure yet lively in a savage, developed yet feeble in civilised man; this truth would have no other consequence than to confirm my argument. Compassion must, in fact, be the stronger, the more the animal beholding any kind of distress identifies himself with the animal that suffers. Now, it is plain that such identification must have been much more perfect in a state of nature than it is in a state of reason. It is reason that engenders self–respect, and reflection that confirms it: it is reason which turns man's mind back upon itself, and divides him from everything that could disturb or afflict him. It is philosophy that isolates him, and bids him say, at sight of the misfortunes of others: "Perish if you will, I am secure." Nothing but such general evils as threaten the whole community can disturb the tranquil sleep of the philosopher, or tear him from his bed. A murder may with impunity be committed under his window; he has only to put his hands to his ears and argue a little with himself, to prevent nature, which is shocked within him, from identifying itself with the unfortunate sufferer. Uncivilised man has not this admirable talent; and for want of reason and wisdom, is always foolishly ready to obey the first promptings of humanity. It is the populace that flocks together at riots and street–brawls, while the wise man prudently makes off. It is the mob and the market–women, who part the combatants, and hinder gentle–folks from cutting one another's throats.

It is then certain that compassion is a natural feeling, which, by moderating the violence of love of self in each individual, contributes to the preservation of the whole species. It is this compassion that hurries us without reflection to the relief of those who are in distress: it is this which in a state of nature supplies the place of laws, morals and virtues, with the advantage that none are tempted to disobey its gentle voice: it is this which will always prevent a sturdy savage from robbing a weak child or a feeble old man of the sustenance they may have with pain and difficulty acquired, if he sees a possibility of providing for himself by other means: it is this which, instead of inculcating that sublime maxim of rational justice. Do to others as you would have them do unto you, inspires all men with that other maxim of natural goodness, much less perfect indeed, but perhaps more useful; Do good to yourself with as little evil as possible to others. In a word, it is rather in this natural feeling than in any subtle arguments that we must look for the cause of that repugnance, which every man would experience in doing evil, even independently of the maxims of education. Although it might belong to Socrates and other minds of the like craft to acquire virtue by reason, the human race would long since have ceased to be, had its preservation depended only on the reasonings of the individuals composing it.

With passions so little active, and so good a curb, men, being rather wild than wicked, and more intent to guard themselves against the mischief that might be done them, than to do mischief to others, were by no means subject to very perilous dissensions. They maintained no kind of intercourse with one another, and were consequently strangers to vanity, deference, esteem and contempt; they had not the least idea of meum and tuum, and no true conception of justice; they looked upon every violence to which they were subjected, rather as an injury that might easily be repaired than as a crime that ought to be punished; and they never thought of taking revenge, unless perhaps mechanically and on the spot, as a dog will sometimes bite the stone which is thrown at him. Their quarrels therefore would seldom have very bloody consequences; for the subject of them would be merely the question of subsistence. But I am aware of one greater danger, which remains to be noticed.

Of the passions that stir the heart of man, there is one which makes the sexes necessary to each other, and is extremely ardent and impetuous; a terrible passion that braves danger, surmounts all obstacles, and in its transports seems calculated to bring destruction on the human race which it is really destined to preserve. What must become of men who are left to this brutal and boundless rage, without modesty, without shame, and daily upholding their amours at the price of their blood?

It must, in the first place, be allowed that, the more violent the passions are, the more are laws necessary to keep them under restraint. But, setting aside the inadequacy of laws to effect this purpose, which is evident from the crimes and disorders to which these passions daily give rise among us, we should do well to inquire if these evils did not spring up with the laws themselves; for in this case, even if the laws were capable of repressing such evils, it is the least that could be expected from them, that they should check a mischief which would not have arisen without them.

Let us begin by distinguishing between the physical and moral ingredients in the feeling of love. The physical part of love is that general desire which urges the sexes to union with each other. The moral part is that which determines and fixes this desire exclusively upon one particular object; or at least gives it a greater degree of energy toward the object thus preferred. It is easy to see that the moral part of love is a factitious feeling, born of social usage, and enhanced by the women with much care and cleverness, to establish their empire, and put in power the sex which ought to obey. This feeling, being founded on certain ideas of beauty and merit which a savage is not in a position to acquire, and on comparisons which he is incapable of making, must be for him almost non-existent; for, as his mind cannot form abstract ideas of proportion and regularity, so his heart is not susceptible of the feelings of love and admiration, which are even insensibly produced by the application of these ideas. He follows solely the character nature has implanted in him, and not tastes which he could never have acquired; so that every woman equally answers his purpose.

Discourse on Inequality

Men in a state of nature being confined merely to what is physical in love, and fortunate enough to be ignorant of those excellences, which whet the appetite while they increase the difficulty of gratifying it, must be subject to fewer and less violent fits of passion, and consequently fall into fewer and less violent disputes. The imagination, which causes such ravages among us, never speaks to the heart of savages, who quietly await the impulses of nature, yield to them involuntarily, with more pleasure than ardour, and, their wants once satisfied, lose the desire. It is therefore incontestable that love, as well as all other passions, must have acquired in society that glowing impetuosity, which makes it so often fatal to mankind. And it is the more absurd to represent savages as continually cutting one another's throats to indulge their brutality, because this opinion is directly contrary to experience; the Caribbeans, who have as yet least of all deviated from the state of nature, being in fact the most peaceable of people in their amours, and the least subject to jealousy, though they live in a hot climate which seems always to inflame the passions.

With regard to the inferences that might be drawn, in the case of several species of animals, the males of which fill our poultry–yards with blood and slaughter, or in spring make the forests resound with their quarrels over their females; we must begin by excluding all those species, in which nature has plainly established, in the comparative power of the sexes, relations different from those which exist among us: thus we can base no conclusion about men on the habits of fighting cocks. In those species where the proportion is better observed, these battles must be entirely due to the scarcity of females in comparison with males; or, what amounts to the same thing, to the intervals during which the female constantly refuses the advances of the male: for if each female admits the male but during two months in the year, it is the same as if the number of females were five–sixths less. Now, neither of these two cases is applicable to the human species, in which the number of females usually exceeds that of males, and among whom it has never been observed, even among savages, that the females have, like those of other animals, their stated times of passion and indifference. Moreover, in several of these species, the individuals all take fire at once, and there comes a fearful moment of universal passion, tumult and disorder among them; a scene which is never beheld in the human species, whose love is not thus seasonal. We must not then conclude from the combats of such animals for the enjoyment of the females, that the case would be the same with mankind in a state of nature: and, even if we drew such a conclusion, we see that such contests do not exterminate other kinds of animals, and we have no reason to think they would be more fatal to ours. It is indeed clear that they would do still less mischief than is the case in a state of society; especially in those countries in which, morals being still held in some repute, the jealousy of lovers and the vengeance of husbands are the daily cause of duels, murders, and even worse crimes; where the obligation of eternal fidelity only occasions adultery, and the very laws of honour and continence necessarily increase debauchery and lead to the multiplication of abortions.

Let us conclude then that man in a state of nature, wandering up and down the forests, without industry, without speech, and without home, an equal stranger to war and to all ties, neither standing in need of his fellow–creatures nor having any desire to hurt them, and perhaps even not distinguishing them one from another; let us conclude that, being self–sufficient and subject to so few passions, he could have no feelings or knowledge but such as befitted his situation; that he felt only his actual necessities, and disregarded everything he did not think himself immediately concerned to notice, and that his understanding made no greater progress than his vanity. If by accident he made any discovery, he was the less able to communicate it to others, as he did not know even his own children. Every art would necessarily perish with its inventor, where there was no kind of education among men, and generations succeeded generations without the least advance; when, all setting out from the same point, centuries must have elapsed in the barbarism of the first ages; when the race was already old, and man remained a child.

If I have expatiated at such length on this supposed primitive state, it is because I had so many ancient errors and inveterate prejudices to eradicate, and therefore thought it incumbent on me to dig down to their very root, and show, by means of a true picture of the state of nature, how far even the natural inequalities of mankind are from having that reality and influence which modern writers suppose.

It is in fact easy to see that many of the differences which distinguish men are merely the effect of habit and the different methods of life men adopt in society. Thus a robust or delicate constitution, and the strength or weakness attaching to it, are more frequently the effects of a hardy or effeminate method of education than of the original endowment of the body. It is the same with the powers of the mind; for education not only makes a difference between such as are cultured and such as are not, but even increases the differences which exist among the former, in proportion to their respective degrees of culture: as the distance between a giant and a dwarf on the same road increases with every step they take. If we compare the prodigious diversity, which obtains in the education and manner of life of the various orders of men in the state of society, with the uniformity and simplicity of animal and savage life, in which every one lives on the same kind of food and in exactly the same manner, and does exactly the same things, it is easy to conceive how much less the difference between man and man must be in a state of nature than in a state of society, and how greatly the natural inequality of mankind must be increased by the inequalities of social institutions.

But even if nature really affected, in the distribution of her gifts, that partiality which is imputed to her, what advantage would the greatest of her favourites derive from it, to the detriment of others, in a state that admits of hardly any kind of relation between them? Where there is no love, of what advantage is beauty? Of what use is wit to those who do not converse, or cunning to those who have no business with others? I hear it constantly repeated that, in such a state, the strong would oppress the weak; but what is here meant by oppression? Some, it is said, would violently domineer over others, who would groan under a servile submission to their caprices. This indeed is exactly what I observe to be the case among us; but I do not see how it can be inferred of men in a state of nature, who could not easily be brought to conceive what we mean by dominion and servitude. One man, it is true, might seize the fruits which another had gathered, the game he had killed, or the cave he had chosen for shelter; but how would he ever be able to exact obedience, and what ties of dependence could there be among men without possessions? If, for instance, I am driven from one tree, I can go to the next; if I am disturbed in one place, what hinders me from going to another? Again, should I happen to meet with a man so much stronger than myself, and at the same time so depraved, so indolent, and so barbarous, as to compel me to provide for his sustenance while he himself remains idle; he must take care not to have his eyes off me for a single moment; he must bind me fast before he goes to sleep, or I shall certainly either knock him on the head or make my escape. That is to say, he must in such a case voluntarily expose himself to much greater trouble than he seeks to avoid, or can give me. After all this, let him be off his guard ever so little; let him but turn his head aside at any sudden noise, and I shall be instantly twenty paces off, lost in the forest, and, my fetters burst asunder, he would never see me again.

Without my expatiating thus uselessly on these details, every one must see that as the bonds of servitude are formed merely by the mutual dependence of men on one another and the reciprocal needs that unite them, it is impossible to make any man a slave, unless he be first reduced to a situation in which he cannot do without the help of others: and, since such a situation does not exist in a state of nature, every one is there his own master, and the law of the strongest is of no effect.

Having proved that the inequality of mankind is hardly felt, and that its influence is next to nothing in a state of nature, I must next show its origin and trace its progress in the successive developments of the human mind. Having shown that human perfectibility, the social virtues, and the other faculties which natural man potentially possessed, could never develop of themselves, but must require the fortuitous concurrence of many foreign causes that might never arise, and without which he would have remained for ever in his primitive condition, I must now collect and consider the different accidents which may have improved the human understanding while depraving the species, and made man wicked while making him sociable; so as to bring him and the world from that distant period to the point at which we now behold them.

I confess that, as the events I am going to describe might have happened in various ways, I have nothing to determine my choice but conjectures: but such conjectures become reasons, when they are the most probable that can be drawn from the nature of things, and the only means of discovering the truth. The consequences, however, which I mean to deduce will not be barely conjectural; as, on the principles just laid down, it would be impossible to form any other theory that would not furnish the same results, and from which I could not draw the same conclusions.

This will be a sufficient apology for my not dwelling on the manner in which the lapse of time compensates for the little probability in the events; on the surprising power of trivial causes, when their action is constant; on the impossibility, on the one hand, of destroying certain hypotheses, though on the other we cannot give them the certainty of known matters of fact; on its being within the province of history, when two facts are given as real, and have to be connected by a series of intermediate facts, which are unknown or supposed to be so, to supply such facts as may connect them; and on its being in the province of philosophy when history is silent, to determine similar facts to serve the same end; and lastly, on the influence of similarity, which, in the case of events, reduces the facts to a much smaller number of different classes than is commonly imagined. It is enough for me to offer these hints to the consideration of my judges, and to have so arranged that the general reader has no need to consider them at all.

THE SECOND PART

THE first man who, having enclosed a piece of ground, bethought himself of saying This is mine, and found people simple enough to believe him, was the real founder of civil society. From how many crimes, wars and murders, from how many horrors and misfortunes might not any one have saved mankind, by pulling up the stakes, or filling up the ditch, and crying to his fellows, "Beware of listening to this impostor; you are undone if you once forget that the fruits of the earth belong to us all, and the earth itself to nobody." But there is great probability that things had then already come to such a pitch, that they could no longer continue as they were; for the idea of property depends on many prior ideas, which could only be acquired successively, and cannot have been formed all at once in the human mind. Mankind must have made very considerable progress, and acquired considerable knowledge and industry which they must also have transmitted and increased from age to age, before they arrived at this last point of the state of nature. Let us then go farther back, and endeavour to unify under a single point of view that slow succession of events and discoveries in the most natural order.

Man's first feeling was that of his own existence, and his first care that of self–preservation. The produce of the earth furnished him with all he needed, and instinct told him how to use it. Hunger and other appetites made him at various times experience various modes of existence; and among these was one which urged him to propagate his species — a blind propensity that, having nothing to do with the heart, produced a merely animal act. The want once gratified, the two sexes knew each other no more; and even the offspring was nothing to its mother, as soon as it could do without her.

Such was the condition of infant man; the life of an animal limited at first to mere sensations, and hardly profiting by the gifts nature bestowed on him, much less capable of entertaining a thought of forcing anything from her. But difficulties soon presented themselves, and it became necessary to learn how to surmount them: the height of the trees, which prevented him from gathering their fruits, the competition of other animals desirous of the same fruits, and the ferocity of those who needed them for their own preservation, all obliged him to apply himself to bodily exercises. He had to be active, swift of foot, and vigorous in fight. Natural weapons, stones and sticks, were easily found: he learnt to surmount the obstacles of nature, to contend in case of necessity with other animals, and to dispute for the means of subsistence even with other men, or to indemnify himself for what he was forced to give up to a stronger.

In proportion as the human race grew more numerous, men's cares increased. The difference of soils, climates and seasons, must have introduced some differences into their manner of living. Barren years, long and sharp winters, scorching summers which parched the fruits of the earth, must have demanded a new industry. On the seashore and the banks of rivers, they invented the hook and line, and became fishermen and eaters of fish. In the forests they made bows and arrows, and became huntsmen and warriors. In cold countries they clothed themselves with the skins of the beasts they had slain. The lightning, a volcano, or some lucky chance acquainted them with fire, a new resource against the rigours of winter: they next learned how to preserve this element, then how to reproduce it, and finally how to prepare with it the flesh of animals which before they had eaten raw.

This repeated relevance of various beings to himself, and one to another, would naturally give rise in the human mind to the perceptions of certain relations between them. Thus the relations which we denote by the terms, great, small, strong, weak, swift, slow, fearful, bold, and the like, almost insensibly compared at need, must have at length produced in him a kind of reflection, or rather a mechanical prudence, which would indicate to him the precautions most necessary to his security.

The new intelligence which resulted from this development increased his superiority over other animals, by making him sensible of it. He would now endeavour, therefore, to ensnare them, would play them a thousand tricks, and though many of them might surpass him in swiftness or in strength, would in time become the master of some and the scourge of others. Thus, the first time he looked into himself, he felt the first emotion of pride; and, at a time when he scarce knew how to distinguish the different orders of beings, by looking upon his species as of the highest order, he prepared the way for assuming pre-eminence as an individual.

Other men, it is true, were not then to him what they now are to us, and he had no greater intercourse with them than with other animals; yet they were not neglected in his observations. The conformities, which he would in time discover between them, and between himself and his female, led him to judge of others which were not then perceptible; and finding that they all behaved as he himself would have done in like circumstances, he naturally inferred that their manner of thinking and acting was altogether in conformity with his own. This important truth, once deeply impressed on his mind, must have induced him, from an intuitive feeling more certain and much more rapid than any kind of reasoning, to pursue the rules of conduct, which he had best observe towards them, for his own security and advantage.

Taught by experience that the love of well−being is the sole motive of human actions, he found himself in a position to distinguish the few cases, in which mutual interest might justify him in relying upon the assistance of his fellows; and also the still fewer cases in which a conflict of interests might give cause to suspect them. In the former case, he joined in the same herd with them, or at most in some kind of loose association, that laid no restraint on its members, and lasted no longer than the transitory occasion that formed it. In the latter case, every one sought his own private advantage, either by open force, if he thought himself strong enough, or by address and cunning, if he felt himself the weaker.

In this manner, men may have insensibly acquired some gross ideas of mutual undertakings, and of the advantages of fulfilling them: that is, just so far as their present and apparent interest was concerned: for they were perfect strangers to foresight, and were so far from troubling themselves about the distant future, that they hardly thought of the morrow. If a deer was to be taken, every one saw that, in order to succeed, he must abide faithfully by his post: but if a hare happened to come within the reach of any one of them, it is not to be doubted that he pursued it without scruple, and, having seized his prey, cared very little, if by so doing he caused his companions to miss theirs.

It is easy to understand that such intercourse would not require a language much more refined than that of rooks or monkeys, who associate together for much the same purpose. Inarticulate cries, plenty of gestures and some imitative sounds, must have been for a long time the universal language; and by the addition, in every country, of some conventional articulate sounds (of which, as I have already intimated, the first institution is not too easy to explain) particular languages were produced; but these were rude and imperfect, and nearly such as are now to be found among some savage nations.

Hurried on by the rapidity of time, by the abundance of things I have to say, and by the almost insensible progress of things in their beginnings, I pass over in an instant a multitude of ages; for the slower the events were in their succession, the more rapidly may they be described.

These first advances enabled men to make others with greater rapidity. In proportion as they grew enlightened, they grew industrious. They ceased to fall asleep under the first tree, or in the first cave that afforded them shelter; they invented several kinds of implements of hard and sharp stones, which they used to dig up the earth, and to cut wood; they then made huts out of branches, and afterwards learnt to plaster them over with mud and clay. This was the epoch of a first revolution, which established and distinguished families, and introduced a kind of property, in itself the source of a thousand quarrels and conflicts. As, however, the strongest were probably the first to build themselves huts which they felt themselves able to defend, it may be concluded that the weak found it much easier and safer to imitate, than to attempt to dislodge them: and of those who were once provided with huts, none could have any inducement to appropriate that of his neighbour; not indeed so much because it did not belong to him, as because it could be of no use, and he could not make himself master of it without exposing himself to a desperate battle with the family which occupied it.

The first expansions of the human heart were the effects of a novel situation, which united husbands and wives, fathers and children, under one roof. The habit of living together soon gave rise to the finest feelings known to humanity, conjugal love and paternal affection. Every family became a little society, the more united because liberty and reciprocal attachment were the only bonds of its union. The sexes, whose manner of life had been hitherto the same, began now to adopt different ways of living. The women became more sedentary, and accustomed themselves to mind the hut and their children, while the men went abroad in search of their common subsistence. From living a softer life, both sexes also began to lose something of their strength and ferocity: but, if individuals became to some extent less able to encounter wild beasts separately, they found it, on the other hand, easier to assemble and resist in common.

The simplicity and solitude of man's life in this new condition, the paucity of his wants, and the implements he had invented to satisfy them, left him a great deal of leisure, which he employed to furnish himself with many conveniences unknown to his fathers: and this was the first yoke he inadvertently imposed on himself, and the first source of the evils he prepared for his descendants. For, besides continuing thus to enervate both body and mind, these conveniences lost with use almost all their power to please, and even degenerated into real needs, till the want of them became far more disagreeable than the possession of them had been pleasant. Men would have been unhappy at the loss of them, though the possession did not make them happy.

Discourse on Inequality

We can here see a little better how the use of speech became established, and insensibly improved in each family, and we may form a conjecture also concerning the manner in which various causes may have extended and accelerated the progress of language, by making it more and more necessary. Floods or earthquakes surrounded inhabited districts with precipices or waters: revolutions of the globe tore off portions from the continent, and made them islands. It is readily seen that among men thus collected and compelled to live together, a common idiom must have arisen much more easily than among those who still wandered through the forests of the continent. Thus it is very possible that after their first essays in navigation the islanders brought over the use of speech to the continent: and it is at least very probable that communities and languages were first established in islands, and even came to perfection there before they were known on the mainland.

Everything now begins to change its aspect. Men, who have up to now been roving in the woods, by taking to a more settled manner of life, come gradually together, form separate bodies, and at length in every country arises a distinct nation, united in character and manners, not by regulations or laws, but by uniformity of life and food, and the common influence of climate. Permanent neighbourhood could not fail to produce, in time, some connection between different families. Among young people of opposite sexes, living in neighbouring huts, the transient commerce required by nature soon led, through mutual intercourse, to another kind not less agreeable, and more permanent. Men began now to take the difference between objects into account, and to make comparisons; they acquired imperceptibly the ideas of beauty and merit, which soon gave rise to feelings of preference. In consequence of seeing each other often, they could not do without seeing each other constantly. A tender and pleasant feeling insinuated itself into their souls, and the least opposition turned it into an impetuous fury: with love arose jealousy; discord triumphed, and human blood was sacrificed to the gentlest of all passions.

As ideas and feelings succeeded one another, and heart and head were brought into play, men continued to lay aside their original wildness; their private connections became every day more intimate as their limits extended. They accustomed themselves to assemble before their huts round a large tree; singing and dancing, the true offspring of love and leisure, became the amusement, or rather the occupation, of men and women thus assembled together with nothing else to do. Each one began to consider the rest, and to wish to be considered in turn; and thus a value came to be attached to public esteem. Whoever sang or danced best, whoever was the handsomest, the strongest, the most dexterous, or the most eloquent, came to be of most consideration; and this was the first step towards inequality, and at the same time towards vice. From these first distinctions arose on the one side vanity and contempt and on the other shame and envy: and the fermentation caused by these new leavens ended by producing combinations fatal to innocence and happiness.

As soon as men began to value one another, and the idea of consideration had got a footing in the mind, every one put in his claim to it, and it became impossible to refuse it to any with impunity. Hence arose the first obligations of civility even among savages; and every intended injury became an affront; because, besides the hurt which might result from it, the party injured was certain to find in it a contempt for his person, which was often more insupportable than the hurt itself.

Thus, as every man punished the contempt shown him by others, in proportion to his opinion of himself, revenge became terrible, and men bloody and cruel. This is precisely the state reached by most of the savage nations known to us: and it is for want of having made a proper distinction in our ideas, and see how very far they already are from the state of nature, that so many writers have hastily concluded that man is naturally cruel, and requires civil institutions to make him more mild; whereas nothing is more gentle than man in his primitive state, as he is placed by nature at an equal distance from the stupidity of brutes, and the fatal ingenuity of civilised man. Equally confined by instinct and reason to the sole care of guarding himself against the mischiefs which threaten him, he is restrained by natural compassion from doing any injury to others, and is not led to do such a thing even in return for injuries received. For, according to the axiom of the wise Locke, There can be no injury, where there is no property.

But it must be remarked that the society thus formed, and the relations thus established among men, required of them qualities different from those which they possessed from their primitive constitution. Morality began to appear in human actions, and every one, before the institution of law, was the only judge and avenger of the injuries done him, so that the goodness which was suitable in the pure state of nature was no longer proper in the new–born state of society. Punishments had to be made more severe, as opportunities of offending became more frequent, and the dread of vengeance had to take the place of the rigour of the law. Thus, though men had become less patient, and their natural compassion had already suffered some diminution, this period of expansion of the human faculties, keeping a just mean between the indolence of the primitive state and the petulant activity of our egoism, must have been the happiest and most stable of epochs.

Discourse on Inequality

The more we reflect on it, the more we shall find that this state was the least subject to revolutions, and altogether the very best man could experience; so that he can have departed from it only through some fatal accident, which, for the public good, should never have happened. The example of savages, most of whom have been found in this state, seems to prove that men were meant to remain in it, that it is the real youth of the world, and that all subsequent advances have been apparently so many steps towards the perfection of the individual, but in reality towards the decrepitude of the species.

So long as men remained content with their rustic huts, so long as they were satisfied with clothes made of the skins of animals and sewn together with thorns and fish–bones, adorned themselves only with feathers and shells, and continued to paint their bodies different colours, to improve and beautify their bows and arrows and to make with sharp–edged stones fishing boats or clumsy musical instruments; in a word, so long as they undertook only what a single person could accomplish, and confined themselves to such arts as did not require the joint labour of several hands, they lived free, healthy, honest and happy lives, so long as their nature allowed, and as they continued to enjoy the pleasures of mutual and independent intercourse. But from the moment one man began to stand in need of the help of another; from the moment it appeared advantageous to any one man to have enough provisions for two, equality disappeared, property was introduced, work became indispensable, and vast forests became smiling fields, which man had to water with the sweat of his brow, and where slavery and misery were soon seen to germinate and grow up with the crops.

Metallurgy and agriculture were the two arts which produced this great revolution. The poets tell us it was gold and silver, but, for the philosophers, it was iron and corn, which first civilised men, and ruined humanity. Thus both were unknown to the savages of America, who for that reason are still savage: the other nations also seem to have continued in a state of barbarism while they practised only one of these arts. One of the best reasons, perhaps, why Europe has been, if not longer, at least more constantly and highly civilised than the rest of the world, is that it is at once the most abundant in iron and the most fertile in corn.

It is difficult to conjecture how men first came to know and use iron; for it is impossible to suppose they would of themselves think of digging the ore out of the mine, and preparing it for smelting, before they knew what would be the result. On the other hand, we have the less reason to suppose this discovery the effect of any accidental fire, as mines are only formed in barren places, bare of trees and plants; so that it looks as if nature had taken pains to keep that fatal secret from us. There remains, therefore, only the extraordinary accident of some volcano which, by ejecting metallic substances already in fusion, suggested to the spectators the idea of imitating the natural operation. And we must further conceive them as possessed of uncommon courage and foresight, to undertake so laborious a work, with so distant a prospect of drawing advantage from it; yet these qualities are united only in minds more advanced than we can suppose those of these first discoverers to have been.

With regard to agriculture, the principles of it were known long before they were put in practice; and it is indeed hardly possible that men, constantly employed in drawing their subsistence from plants and trees, should not readily acquire a knowledge of the means made use of by nature for the propagation of vegetables. It was in all probability very long, however, before their industry took that turn, either because trees, which together with hunting and fishing afforded them food, did not require their attention; or because they were ignorant of the use of corn, or without instruments to cultivate it; or because they lacked foresight to future needs; or lastly, because they were without means of preventing others from robbing them of the fruit of their labour.

When they grew more industrious, it is natural to believe that they began, with the help of sharp stones and pointed sticks, to cultivate a few vegetables or roots around their huts; though it was long before they knew how to prepare corn, or were provided with the implements necessary for raising it in any large quantity; not to mention how essential it is, for husbandry, to consent to immediate loss, in order to reap a future gain — a precaution very foreign to the turn of a savage's mind; for, as I have said, he hardly foresees in the morning what he will need at night.

The invention of the other arts must therefore have been necessary to compel mankind to apply themselves to agriculture. No sooner were artificers wanted to smelt and forge iron, than others were required to maintain them; the more hands that were employed in manufactures, the fewer were left to provide for the common subsistence, though the number of mouths to be furnished with food remained the same: and as some required commodities in exchange for their iron, the rest at length discovered the method of making iron serve for the multiplication of commodities. By this means the arts of husbandry and agriculture were established on the one hand, and the art of working metals and multiplying their uses on the other.

Discourse on Inequality

The cultivation of the earth necessarily brought about its distribution; and property, once recognised, gave rise to the first rules of justice; for, to secure each man his own, it had to be possible for each to have something. Besides, as men began to look forward to the future, and all had something to lose, every one had reason to apprehend that reprisals would follow any injury he might do to another. This origin is so much the more natural, as it is impossible to conceive how property can come from anything but manual labour: for what else can a man add to things which he does not originally create, so as to make them his own property? It is the husbandman's labour alone that, giving him a title to the produce of the ground he has tilled, gives him a claim also to the land itself, at least till harvest, and so, from year to year, a constant possession which is easily transformed into property. When the ancients, says Grotius, gave to Ceres the title of Legislatrix, and to a festival celebrated in her honour the name of Thesmophoria, they meant by that that the distribution of lands had produced a new kind of right: that is to say, the right of property, which is different from the right deducible from the law of nature.

In this state of affairs, equality might have been sustained, had the talents of individuals been equal, and had, for example, the use of iron and the consumption of commodities always exactly balanced each other; but, as there was nothing to preserve this balance, it was soon disturbed; the strongest did most work; the most skilful turned his labour to best account; the most ingenious devised methods of diminishing his labour: the husbandman wanted more iron, or the smith more corn, and, while both laboured equally, the one gained a great deal by his work, while the other could hardly support himself. Thus natural inequality unfolds itself insensibly with that of combination, and the difference between men, developed by their different circumstances, becomes more sensible and permanent in its effects, and begins to have an influence, in the same proportion, over the lot of individuals.

Matters once at this pitch, it is easy to imagine the rest. I shall not detain the reader with a description of the successive invention of other arts, the development of language, the trial and utilisation of talents, the inequality of fortunes, the use and abuse of riches, and all the details connected with them which the reader can easily supply for himself. I shall confine myself to a glance at mankind in this new situation.

Behold then all human faculties developed, memory and imagination in full play, egoism interested, reason active, and the mind almost at the highest point of its perfection. Behold all the natural qualities in action, the rank and condition of every man assigned him; not merely his share of property and his power to serve or injure others, but also his wit, beauty, strength or skill, merit or talents: and these being the only qualities capable of commanding respect, it soon became necessary to possess or to affect them.

It now became the interest of men to appear what they really were not. To be and to seem became two totally different things; and from this distinction sprang insolent pomp and cheating trickery, with all the numerous vices that go in their train. On the other hand, free and independent as men were before, they were now, in consequence of a multiplicity of new wants, brought into subjection, as it were, to all nature, and particularly to one another; and each became in some degree a slave even in becoming the master of other men: if rich, they stood in need of the services of others; if poor, of their assistance; and even a middle condition did not enable them to do without one another. Man must now, therefore, have been perpetually employed in getting others to interest themselves in his lot, and in making them, apparently at least, if not really, find their advantage in promoting his own. Thus he must have been sly and artful in his behaviour to some, and imperious and cruel to others; being under a kind of necessity to ill−use all the persons of whom he stood in need, when he could not frighten them into compliance, and did not judge it his interest to be useful to them. Insatiable ambition, the thirst of raising their respective fortunes, not so much from real want as from the desire to surpass others, inspired all men with a vile propensity to injure one another, and with a secret jealousy, which is the more dangerous, as it puts on the mask of benevolence, to carry its point with greater security. In a word, there arose rivalry and competition on the one hand, and conflicting interests on the other, together with a secret desire on both of profiting at the expense of others. All these evils were the first effects of property, and the inseparable attendants of growing inequality.

Before the invention of signs to represent riches, wealth could hardly consist in anything but lands and cattle, the only real possessions men can have. But, when inheritances so increased in number and extent as to occupy the whole of the land, and to border on one another, one man could aggrandise himself only at the expense of another; at the same time the supernumeraries, who had been too weak or too indolent to make such acquisitions, and had grown poor without sustaining any loss, because, while they saw everything change around them, they remained still the same, were obliged to receive their subsistence, or steal it, from the rich; and this soon bred, according to their different characters, dominion and slavery, or violence and rapine. The wealthy, on their part, had no sooner begun to taste the pleasure of command, than they disdained all others, and, using their old slaves to acquire new, thought of nothing but subduing and enslaving their neighbours; like ravenous wolves, which, having once tasted human flesh, despise every other food and thenceforth seek only men to devour.

Thus, as the most powerful or the most miserable considered their might or misery as a kind of right to the possessions of others, equivalent, in their opinion, to that of property, the destruction of equality was attended by the most terrible disorders. Usurpations by the rich, robbery by the poor, and the unbridled passions of both, suppressed the cries of natural compassion and the still feeble voice of justice, and filled men with avarice, ambition and vice. Between the title of the strongest and that of the first occupier, there arose perpetual conflicts, which never ended but in battles and bloodshed. The new-born state of society thus gave rise to a horrible state of war; men thus harassed and depraved were no longer capable of retracing their steps or renouncing the fatal acquisitions they had made, but, labouring by the abuse of the faculties which do them honour, merely to their own confusion, brought themselves to the brink of ruin.

Attonitus novitate mali, divesque miserque, Effugere optat opes; et quæ modo voverat odit.[5]

It is impossible that men should not at length have reflected on so wretched a situation, and on the calamities that overwhelmed them. The rich, in particular, must have felt how much they suffered by a constant state of war, of which they bore all the expense; and in which, though all risked their lives, they alone risked their property. Besides, however speciously they might disguise their usurpations, they knew that they were founded on precarious and false titles; so that, if others took from them by force what they themselves had gained by force, they would have no reason to complain. Even those who had been enriched by their own industry, could hardly base their proprietorship on better claims. It was in vain to repeat, "I built this well; I gained this spot by my industry." Who gave you your standing, it might be answered, and what right have you to demand payment of us for doing what we never asked you to do? Do you not know that numbers of your fellow-creatures are starving, for want of what you have too much of? You ought to have had the express and universal consent of mankind, before appropriating more of the common subsistence than you needed for your own maintenance. Destitute of valid reasons to justify and sufficient strength to defend himself, able to crush individuals with ease, but easily crushed himself by a troop of bandits, one against all, and incapable, on account of mutual jealousy, of joining with his equals against numerous enemies united by the common hope of plunder, the rich man, thus urged by necessity, conceived at length the profoundest plan that ever entered the mind of man: this was to employ in his favour the forces of those who attacked him, to make allies of his adversaries, to inspire them with different maxims, and to give them other institutions as favourable to himself as the law of nature was unfavourable.

With this view, after having represented to his neighbours the horror of a situation which armed every man against the rest, and made their possessions as burdensome to them as their wants, and in which no safety could be expected either in riches or in poverty, he readily devised plausible arguments to make them close with his design. "Let us join," said he, "to guard the weak from oppression, to restrain the ambitious, and secure to every man the possession of what belongs to him: let us institute rules of justice and peace, to which all without exception may be obliged to conform; rules that may in some measure make amends for the caprices of fortune, by subjecting equally the powerful and the weak to the observance of reciprocal obligations. Let us, in a word, instead of turning our forces against ourselves, collect them in a supreme power which may govern us by wise laws, protect and defend all the members of the association, repulse their common enemies, and maintain eternal harmony among us."

Far fewer words to this purpose would have been enough to impose on men so barbarous and easily seduced; especially as they had too many disputes among themselves to do without arbitrators, and too much ambition and avarice to go long without masters. All ran headlong to their chains, in hopes of securing their liberty; for they had just wit enough to perceive the advantages of political institutions, without experience enough to enable them to foresee the dangers. The most capable of foreseeing the dangers were the very persons who expected to benefit by them; and even the most prudent judged it not inexpedient to sacrifice one part of their freedom to ensure the rest; as a wounded man has his arm cut off to save the rest of his body.

Such was, or may well have been, the origin of society and law, which bound new fetters on the poor, and gave new powers to the rich; which irretrievably destroyed natural liberty, eternally fixed the law of property and inequality, converted clever usurpation into unalterable right, and, for the advantage of a few ambitious individuals, subjected all mankind to perpetual labour, slavery and wretchedness. It is easy to see how the establishment of one community made that of all the rest necessary, and how, in order to make head against united forces, the rest of mankind had to unite in turn. Societies soon multiplied and spread over the face of the earth, till hardly a corner of the world was left in which a man could escape the yoke, and withdraw his head from beneath the sword which he saw perpetually hanging over him by a thread. Civil right having thus become the common rule among the members of each community, the law of nature maintained its place only between different communities, where, under the name of the right of nations, it was qualified by certain tacit conventions, in order to make commerce practicable, and serve as a substitute for natural compassion, which lost, when applied to societies, almost all the influence it had over individuals, and survived no longer except in some great cosmopolitan spirits, who, breaking down the imaginary barriers that separate different peoples, follow the example of our Sovereign Creator, and include the whole human race in their benevolence.

But bodies politic, remaining thus in a state of nature among themselves, presently experienced the inconveniences which had obliged individuals to forsake it; for this state became still more fatal to these great bodies than it had been to the individuals of whom they were composed. Hence arose national wars, battles, murders, and reprisals, which shock nature and outrage reason; together with all those horrible prejudices which class among the virtues the honour of shedding human blood. The most distinguished men hence learned to consider cutting each other's throats a duty; at length men massacred their fellow–creatures by thousands without so much as knowing why, and committed more murders in a single day's fighting, and more violent outrages in the sack of a single town, than were committed in the state of nature during whole ages over the whole earth. Such were the first effects which we can see to have followed the division of mankind into different communities. But let us return to their institutions.

I know that some writers have given other explanations of the origin of political societies, such as the conquest of the powerful, or the association of the weak. It is, indeed, indifferent to my argument which of these causes we choose. That which I have just laid down, however, appears to me the most natural for the following reasons. First: because, in the first case, the right of conquest, being no right in itself, could not serve as a foundation on which to build any other; the victor and the vanquished people still remained with respect to each other in the state of war, unless the vanquished, restored to the full possession of their liberty, voluntarily made choice of the victor for their chief. For till then, whatever capitulation may have been made being founded on violence, and therefore ipso facto void, there could not have been on this hypothesis either a real society or body politic, or any law other than that of the strongest. Secondly: because the words strong and weak are, in the second case, ambiguous; for during the interval between the establishment of a right of property, or prior occupancy, and that of political government, the meaning of these words is better expressed by the terms rich and poor: because, in fact, before the institution of laws, men had no other way of reducing their equals to submission, than by attacking their goods, or making some of their own over to them. Thirdly: because, as the poor had nothing but their freedom to lose, it would have been in the highest degree absurd for them to resign voluntarily the only good they still enjoyed, without getting anything in exchange: whereas the rich having feelings, if I may so express myself, in every part of their possessions, it was much easier to harm them, and therefore more necessary for them to take precautions against it; and, in short, because it is more reasonable to suppose a thing to have been invented by those to whom it would be of service, than by those whom it must have harmed.

Government had, in its infancy, no regular and constant form. The want of experience and philosophy prevented men from seeing any but present inconveniences, and they thought of providing against others only as they presented themselves. In spite of the endeavours of the wisest legislators, the political state remained imperfect, because it was little more than the work of chance; and, as it had begun ill, though time revealed its defects and suggested remedies, the original faults were never repaired. It was continually being patched up, when the first task should have been to get the site cleared and all the old materials removed, as was done by Lycurgus at Sparta, if a stable and lasting edifice was to be erected. Society consisted at first merely of a few general conventions, which every member bound himself to observe; and for the performance of covenants the whole body went security to each individual. Experience only could show the weakness of such a constitution, and how easily it might be infringed with impunity, from the difficulty of convicting men of faults, where the public alone was to be witness and judge: the laws could not but be eluded in many ways; disorders and inconveniences could not but multiply continually, till it became necessary to commit the dangerous trust of public authority to private persons, and the care of enforcing obedience to the deliberations of the people to the magistrate. For to say that chiefs were chosen before the confederacy was formed, and that the administrators of the laws were there before the laws themselves, is too absurd a supposition to consider seriously.

It would be as unreasonable to suppose that men at first threw themselves irretrievably and unconditionally into the arms of an absolute master, and that the first expedient which proud and unsubdued men hit upon for their common security was to run headlong into slavery. For what reason, in fact, did they take to themselves superiors, if it was not in order that they might be defended from oppression, and have protection for their lives, liberties and properties, which are, so to speak, the constituent elements of their being? Now, in the relations between man and man, the worst that can happen is for one to find himself at the mercy of another, and it would have been inconsistent with common–sense to begin by bestowing on a chief the only things they wanted his help to preserve. What equivalent could he offer them for so great a right? And if he had presumed to exact it under pretext of defending them, would he not have received the answer recorded in the fable: "What more can the enemy do to us?" It is therefore beyond dispute, and indeed the fundamental maxim of all political right, that people have set up chiefs to protect their liberty, and not to enslave them. If we have a prince, said Pliny to Trajan, it is to save ourselves from having a master.

Politicians indulge in the same sophistry about the love of liberty as philosophers about the state of nature. They judge, by what they see, of very different things, which they have not seen; and attribute to man a natural propensity to servitude, because the slaves within their observation are seen to bear the yoke with patience; they fail to reflect that it is with liberty as with innocence and virtue; the value is known only to those who possess them, and the taste for them is forfeited when they are forfeited themselves. "I know the charms of your country," said Brasidas to a satrap, who was comparing the life at Sparta with that at Persepolis, "but you cannot know the pleasures of mine."

An unbroken horse erects his mane, paws the ground and starts back impetuously at the sight of the bridle; while one which is properly trained suffers patiently even whip and spur: so savage man will not bend his neck to the yoke to which civilised man submits without a murmur, but prefers the most turbulent state of liberty to the most peaceful slavery. We cannot therefore, from the servility of nations already enslaved, judge of the natural disposition of mankind for or against slavery; we should go by the prodigious efforts of every free people to save itself from oppression. I know that the former are for ever holding forth in praise of the tranquillity they enjoy in their chains, and that they call a state of wretched servitude a state of peace: miserrimam servitutem pacem appellant.[6] But when I observe the latter sacrificing pleasure, peace, wealth, power and life itself to the preservation of that one treasure, which is so disdained by those who have lost it; when I see free–born animals dash their brains out against the bars of their cage, from an innate impatience of captivity; when I behold numbers of naked savages, that despise European pleasures, braving hunger, fire, the sword and death, to preserve nothing but their independence, I feel that it is not for slaves to argue about liberty.

With regard to paternal authority, from which some writers have derived absolute government and all society, it is enough, without going back to the contrary arguments of Locke and Sidney, to remark that nothing on earth can be further from the ferocious spirit of despotism than the mildness of that authority which looks more to the advantage of him who obeys than to that of him who commands; that, by the law of nature, the father is the child's master no longer than his help is necessary; that from that time they are both equal, the son being perfectly independent of the father, and owing him only respect and not obedience. For gratitude is a duty which ought to be paid, but not a right to be exacted: instead of saying that civil society is derived from paternal authority, we ought to say rather that the latter derives its principal force from the former. No individual was ever acknowledged as the father of many, till his sons and daughters remained settled around him. The goods of the father, of which he is really the master, are the ties which keep his children in dependence, and he may bestow on them, if he pleases, no share of his property, unless they merit it by constant deference to his will. But the subjects of an arbitrary despot are so far from having the like favour to expect from their chief, that they themselves and everything they possess are his property, or at least are considered by him as such; so that they are forced to receive, as a favour, the little of their own he is pleased to leave them. When he despoils them, he does but justice, and mercy in that he permits them to live.

By proceeding thus to test fact by right, we should discover as little reason as truth in the voluntary establishment of tyranny. It would also be no easy matter to prove the validity of a contract binding on only one of the parties, where all the risk is on one side, and none on the other; so that no one could suffer but he who bound himself. This hateful system is indeed, even in modern times, very far from being that of wise and good monarchs, and especially of the kings of France; as may be seen from several passages in their edicts; particularly from the following passage in a celebrated edict published in 1667 in the name and by order of Louis XIV.

"Let it not, therefore, be said that the Sovereign is not subject to the laws of his State; since the contrary is a true proposition of the right of nations, which flattery has sometimes attacked but good princes have always defended as the tutelary divinity of their dominions. How much more legitimate is it to say with the wise Plato, that the perfect felicity of a kingdom consists in the obedience of subjects to their prince, and of the prince to the laws, and in the laws being just and constantly directed to the public good!"[7]

I shall not stay here to inquire whether, as liberty is the noblest faculty of man, it is not degrading our very nature, reducing ourselves to the level of the brutes, which are mere slaves of instinct, and even an affront to the Author of our being, to renounce without reserve the most precious of all His gifts, and to bow to the necessity of committing all the crimes He has forbidden, merely to gratify a mad or a cruel master; or if this sublime craftsman ought not to be less angered at seeing His workmanship entirely destroyed than thus dishonoured. I will waive (if my opponents please) the authority of Barbeyrac, who, following Locke, roundly declares that no man can so far sell his liberty as to submit to an arbitrary power which may use him as it likes. For, he adds, this would be to sell his own life, of which he is not master. I shall ask only what right those who were not afraid thus to debase themselves could have to subject their posterity to the same ignominy, and to renounce for them those blessings which they do not owe to the liberality of their progenitors, and without which life itself must be a burden to all who are worthy of it.

Puffendorf says that we may divest ourselves of our liberty in favour of other men, just as we transfer our property from one to another by contracts and agreements. But this seems a very weak argument. For in the first place, the property I alienate becomes quite foreign to me, nor can I suffer from the abuse of it; but it very nearly concerns me that my liberty should not be abused, and I cannot without incurring the guilt of the crimes I may be compelled to commit, expose myself to become an instrument of crime. Besides, the right of property being only a convention of human institution, men may dispose of what they possess as they please: but this is not the case with the essential gifts of nature, such as life and liberty, which every man is permitted to enjoy, and of which it is at least doubtful whether any have a right to divest themselves. By giving up the one, we degrade our being; by giving up the other, we do our best to annul it; and, as no temporal good can indemnify us for the loss of either, it would be an offence against both reason and nature to renounce them at any price whatsoever. But, even if we could transfer our liberty, as we do our property, there would be a great difference with regard to the children, who enjoy the father's substance only by the transmission of his right; whereas, liberty being a gift which they hold from nature as being men, their parents have no right whatever to deprive them of it. As then, to establish slavery, it was necessary to do violence to nature, so, in order to perpetuate such a right, nature would have to be changed. Jurists, who have gravely determined that the child of a slave comes into the world a slave, have decided, in other words, that a man shall come into the world not a man.

I regard it then as certain, that government did not begin with arbitrary power, but that this is the depravation, the extreme term, of government, and brings it back, finally, to just the law of the strongest, which it was originally designed to remedy. Supposing, however, it had begun in this manner, such power, being in itself illegitimate, could not have served as a basis for the laws of society, nor, consequently, for the inequality they instituted.

Without entering at present upon the investigations which still remain to be made into the nature of the fundamental compact underlying all government, I content myself with adopting the common opinion concerning it, and regard the establishment of the political body as a real contract between the people and the chiefs chosen by them: a contract by which both parties bind themselves to observe the laws therein expressed, which form the ties of their union. The people having in respect of their social relations concentrated all their wills in one, the several articles, concerning which this will is explained, become so many fundamental laws, obligatory on all the members of the State without exception, and one of these articles regulates the choice and power of the magistrates appointed to watch over the execution of the rest. This power extends to everything which may maintain the constitution, without going so far as to alter it. It is accompanied by honours, in order to bring the laws and their administrators into respect. The ministers are also distinguished by personal prerogatives, in order to recompense them for the cares and labour which good administration involves. The magistrate, on his side, binds himself to use the power he is entrusted with only in conformity with the intention of his constituents, to maintain them all in the peaceable possession of what belongs to them, and to prefer on every occasion the public interest to his own.

Before experience had shown, or knowledge of the human heart enabled men to foresee, the unavoidable abuses of such a constitution, it must have appeared so much the more excellent, as those who were charged with the care of its preservation had themselves most interest in it; for magistracy and the rights attaching to it being based solely on the fundamental laws, the magistrates would cease to be legitimate as soon as these ceased to exist; the people would no longer owe them obedience; and as not the magistrates, but the laws, are essential to the being of a State, the members of it would regain the right to their natural liberty.

Discourse on Inequality

If we reflect with ever so little attention on this subject, we shall find new arguments to confirm this truth, and be convinced from the very nature of the contract that it cannot be irrevocable: for, if there were no superior power capable of ensuring the fidelity of the contracting parties, or compelling them to perform their reciprocal engagements, the parties would be sole judges in their own cause, and each would always have a right to renounce the contract, as soon as he found that the other had violated its terms, or that they no longer suited his convenience. It is upon this principle that the right of abdication may possibly be founded. Now, if, as here, we consider only what is human in this institution, it is certain that, if the magistrate, who has all the power in his own hands, and appropriates to himself all the advantages of the contract, has none the less a right to renounce his authority, the people, who suffer for all the faults of their chief, must have a much better right to renounce their dependence. But the terrible and innumerable quarrels and disorders that would necessarily arise from so dangerous a privilege, show, more than anything else, how much human government stood in need of a more solid basis than mere reason, and how expedient it was for the public tranquillity that the divine will should interpose to invest the sovereign authority with a sacred and inviolable character, which might deprive subjects of the fatal right of disposing of it. If the world had received no other advantages from religion, this would be enough to impose on men the duty of adopting and cultivating it, abuses and all, since it has been the means of saving more blood than fanaticism has ever spilt. But let us follow the thread of our hypothesis.

The different forms of government owe their origin to the differing degrees of inequality which existed between individuals at the time of their institution. If there happened to be any one man among them pre–eminent in power, virtue, riches or personal influence, he became sole magistrate, and the State assumed the form of monarchy. If several, nearly equal in point of eminence, stood above the rest, they were elected jointly, and formed an aristocracy. Again, among a people who had deviated less from a state of nature, and between whose fortune or talents there was less disproportion, the supreme administration was retained in common, and a democracy was formed. It was discovered in process of time which of these forms suited men the best. Some peoples remained altogether subject to the laws; others soon came to obey their magistrates. The citizens laboured to preserve their liberty; the subjects, irritated at seeing others enjoying a blessing they had lost, thought only of making slaves of their neighbours. In a word, on the one side arose riches and conquests, and on the other happiness and virtue.

In these different governments, all the offices were at first elective; and when the influence of wealth was out of the question, the preference was given to merit, which gives a natural ascendancy, and to age, which is experienced in business and deliberate in council. The Elders of the Hebrews, the Gerontes at Sparta, the Senate at Rome, and the very etymology of our word Seigneur, show how old age was once held in veneration. But the more often the choice fell upon old men, the more often elections had to be repeated, and the more they became a nuisance; intrigues set in, factions were formed, party feeling grew bitter, civil wars broke out; the lives of individuals were sacrificed to the pretended happiness of the State; and at length men were on the point of relapsing into their primitive anarchy. Ambitious chiefs profited by these circumstances to perpetuate their offices in their own families: at the same time the people, already used to dependence, ease, and the conveniences of life, and already incapable of breaking its fetters, agreed to an increase of its slavery, in order to secure its tranquillity. Thus magistrates, having become hereditary, contracted the habit of considering their offices as a family estate, and themselves as proprietors of the communities of which they were at first only the officers, of regarding their fellow–citizens as their slaves, and numbering them, like cattle, among their belongings, and of calling themselves the equals of the gods and kings of kings.

If we follow the progress of inequality in these various revolutions, we shall find that the establishment of laws and of the right of property was its first term, the institution of magistracy the second, and the conversion of legitimate into arbitrary power the third and last; so that the condition of rich and poor was authorised by the first period; that of powerful and weak by the second; and only by the third that of master and slave, which is the last degree of inequality, and the term at which all the rest remain, when they have got so far, till the government is either entirely dissolved by new revolutions, or brought back again to legitimacy.

To understand this progress as necessary we must consider not so much the motives for the establishment of the body politic, as the forms it assumes in actuality, and the faults that necessarily attend it: for the flaws which make social institutions necessary are the same as make the abuse of them unavoidable. If we except Sparta, where the laws were mainly concerned with the education of children, and where Lycurgus established such morality as practically made laws needles — for laws as a rule, being weaker than the passions, restrain men without altering them — it would not be difficult to prove that every government, which scrupulously complied with the ends for which it was instituted, and guarded carefully against change and corruption, was set up unnecessarily. For a country, in which no one either evaded the laws or made a bad use of magisterial power, could require neither laws nor magistrates.

Political distinctions necessarily produce civil distinctions. The growing equality between the chiefs and the people is soon felt by individuals, and modified in a thousand ways according to passions, talents and circumstances. The magistrate could not usurp any illegitimate power, without giving distinction to the creatures with whom he must share it. Besides, individuals only allow themselves to be oppressed so far as they are hurried on by blind ambition, and, looking rather below than above them, come to love authority more than independence, and submit to slavery, that they may in turn enslave others. It is no easy matter to reduce to obedience a man who has no ambition to command; nor would the most adroit politician find it possible to enslave a people whose only desire was to be independent. But inequality easily makes its way among cowardly and ambitious minds, which are ever ready to run the risks of fortune, and almost indifferent whether they command or obey, as it is favourable or adverse. Thus, there must have been a time, when the eyes of the people were so fascinated, that their rules had only to say to the least of men, "Be great, you and all your posterity," to make him immediately appear great in the eyes of every one as well as in his own. His descendants took still more upon them, in proportion to their distance from him; the more obscure and uncertain the cause, the greater the effect: the greater the number of idlers one could count in a family, the more illustrious it was held to be.

If this were the place to go into details, I could readily explain how, even without the intervention of government, inequality of credit and authority became unavoidable among private persons, as soon as their union in a single society made them compare themselves one with another, and take into account the differences which they found out from the continual intercourse every man had to have with his neighbours.[8] These differences are of several kinds; but riches, nobility or rank, power and personal merit being the principal distinctions by which men form an estimate of each other in society, I could prove that the harmony or conflict of these different forces is the surest indication of the good or bad constitution of a State. I could show that among these four kinds of inequality, personal qualities being the origin of all the others, wealth is the one to which they are all reduced in the end; for, as riches tend most immediately to the prosperity of individuals, and are easiest to communicate, they are used to purchase every other distinction. By this observation we are enabled to judge pretty exactly how far a people has departed from its primitive constitution, and of its progress towards the extreme term of corruption. I could explain how much this universal desire for reputation, honours and advancement, which inflames us all, exercises and holds up to comparison our faculties and powers; how it excites and multiplies our passions, and, by creating universal competition and rivalry, or rather enmity, among men, occasions numberless failures, successes and disturbances of all kinds by making so many aspirants run the same course. I could show that it is to this desire of being talked about, and this unremitting rage of distinguishing ourselves, that we owe the best and the worst things we possess, both our virtues and our vices, our science and our errors, our conquerors and our philosophers; that is to say, a great many bad things, and a very few good ones. In a word, I could prove that, if we have a few rich and powerful men on the pinnacle of fortune and grandeur, while the crowd grovels in want and obscurity, it is because the former prize what they enjoy only in so far as others are destitute of it; and because, without changing their condition, they would cease to be happy the moment the people ceased to be wretched.

These details alone, however, would furnish matter for a considerable work, in which the advantages and disadvantages of every kind of government might be weighed, as they are related to man in the state of nature, and at the same time all the different aspects, under which inequality has up to the present appeared, or may appear in ages yet to come, according to the nature of the several governments, and the alterations which time must unavoidably occasion in them, might be demonstrated. We should then see the multitude oppressed from within, in consequence of the very precautions it had taken to guard against foreign tyranny. We should see oppression continually gain ground without it being possible for the oppressed to know where it would stop, or what legitimate means was left them of checking its progress. We should see the rights of citizens, and the freedom of nations slowly extinguished, and the complaints, protests and appeals of the weak treated as seditious murmurings. We should see the honour of defending the common cause confined by statecraft to a mercenary part of the people. We should see taxes made necessary by such means, and the disheartened husbandman deserting his fields even in the midst of peace, and leaving the plough to gird on the sword. We should see fatal and capricious codes of honour established; and the champions of their country sooner or later becoming its enemies, and for ever holding their daggers to the breasts of their fellow-citizens. The time would come when they would be heard saying to the oppressor of their country —

Discourse on Inequality

Pectore si fratris gladium juguloque parentis Condere me jubeas, gravidæque in viscera partu Conjugis, invita peragam tamen omnia dextrâ. Lucan, i. 376

From great inequality of fortunes and conditions, from the vast variety of passions and of talents, of useless and pernicious arts, of vain sciences, would arise a multitude of prejudices equally contrary to reason, happiness and virtue. We should see the magistrates fomenting everything that might weaken men united in society, by promoting dissension among them; everything that might sow in it the seeds of actual division, while it gave society the air of harmony; everything that might inspire the different ranks of people with mutual hatred and distrust, by setting the rights and interests of one against those of another, and so strengthen the power which comprehended them all.

It is from the midst of this disorder and these revolutions, that despotism, gradually raising up its hideous head and devouring everything that remained sound and untainted in any part of the State, would at length trample on both the laws and the people, and establish itself on the ruins of the republic. The times which immediately preceded this last change would be times of trouble and calamity; but at length the monster would swallow up everything, and the people would no longer have either chiefs or laws, but only tyrants. From this moment there would be no question of virtue or morality; for despotism cui ex honesto nulla est spes, wherever it prevails, admits no other master; it no sooner speaks than probity and duty lose their weight and blind obedience is the only virtue which slaves can still practise.

This is the last term of inequality, the extreme point that closes the circle, and meets that from which we set out. Here all private persons return to their first equality, because they are nothing; and, subjects having no law but the will of their master, and their master no restraint but his passions, all notions of good and all principles of equity again vanish. There is here a complete return to the law of the strongest, and so to a new state of nature, differing from that we set out from; for the one was a state of nature in its first purity, while this is the consequence of excessive corruption. There is so little difference between the two states in other respects, and the contract of government is so completely dissolved by despotism, that the despot is master only so long as he remains the strongest; as soon as he can be expelled, he has no right to complain of violence. The popular insurrection that ends in the death or deposition of a Sultan is as lawful an act as those by which he disposed, the day before, of the lives and fortunes of his subjects. As he was maintained by force alone, it is force alone that overthrows him. Thus everything takes place according to the natural order; and, whatever may be the result of such frequent and precipitate revolutions, no one man has reason to complain of the injustice of another, but only of his own ill-fortune or indiscretion.

If the reader thus discovers and retraces the lost and forgotten road, by which man must have passed from the state of nature to the state of society; if he carefully restores, along with the intermediate situations which I have just described, those which want of time has compelled me to suppress, or my imagination has failed to suggest, he cannot fail to be struck by the vast distance which separates the two states. It is in tracing this slow succession that he will find the solution of a number of problems of politics and morals, which philosophers cannot settle. He will feel that, men being different in different ages, the reason why Diogenes could not find a man was that he sought among his contemporaries a man of an earlier period. He will see that Cato died with Rome and liberty, because he did not fit the age in which he lived; the greatest of men served only to astonish a world which he would certainly have ruled, had he lived five hundred years sooner. In a word, he will explain how the soul and the passions of men insensibly change their very nature; why our wants and pleasures in the end seek new objects; and why, the original man having vanished by degrees, society offers to us only an assembly of artificial men and factitious passions, which are the work of all these new relations, and without any real foundation in nature. We are taught nothing on this subject, by reflection, that is not entirely confirmed by observation. The savage and the civilised man differ so much in the bottom of their hearts and in their inclinations, that what constitutes the supreme happiness of one would reduce the other to despair. The former breathes only peace and liberty; he desires only to live and be free from labour; even the ataraxia of the Stoic falls far short of his profound indifference to every other object. Civilised man, on the other hand, is always moving, sweating, toiling and racking his brains to find still more laborious occupations: he goes on in drudgery to his last moment, and even seeks death to put himself in a position to live, or renounces life to acquire immortality. He pays his court to men in power, whom he hates, and to the wealthy, whom he despises; he stops at nothing to have the honour of serving them; he is not ashamed to value himself on his own meanness and their protection; and, proud of his slavery, he speaks with disdain of those, who have not the honour of sharing it. What a sight would the perplexing and envied labours of a European minister of State present to the eyes of a Caribbean! How many cruel deaths would not this indolent savage prefer to the horrors of such a life, which is seldom even sweetened by the pleasure of doing good! But, for him to see into the motives of all this solicitude, the words power and reputation, would have to bear some meaning in his mind; he would have to know that there are men who set a value on the opinion of the rest of the world; who can be made happy and satisfied with themselves rather on the testimony of other people than on their own. In reality, the source of all these differences is, that the savage lives within himself, while social man lives constantly outside himself, and only knows how to live in the opinion of others, so that he seems to receive the consciousness of his own existence merely from the judgment of others concerning him. It is not to my present purpose to insist on the indifference to good and evil which arises from this disposition, in spite of our many fine works on morality, or to show how, everything being reduced to appearances, there is but art and mummery in even honour, friendship, virtue, and often vice itself, of which we at length learn the secret of boasting; to show, in short, how, always asking others what we are, and never daring to ask ourselves, in the midst of so much philosophy, humanity and civilisation, and of such sublime codes of morality, we have nothing to show for ourselves but a frivolous and deceitful appearance, honour without virtue, reason without wisdom, and pleasure without happiness. It is sufficient that I have proved that this is not by any means the original state of man, but that it is merely the spirit of society, and the inequality which society produces, that thus transform and alter all our natural inclinations.

I have endeavoured to trace the origin and progress of inequality, and the institution and abuse of political societies, as far as these are capable of being deduced from the nature of man merely by the light of reason, and independently of those sacred dogmas which give the sanction of divine right to sovereign authority. It follows from this survey that, as there is hardly any inequality in the state of nature, all the inequality which now prevails owes its strength and growth to the development of our faculties and the advance of the human mind, and becomes at last permanent and legitimate by the establishment of property and laws. Secondly, it follows that moral inequality, authorised by positive right alone, clashes with natural right, whenever it is not proportionate to physical inequality; a distinction which sufficiently determines what we ought to think of that species of inequality which prevails in all civilised, countries; since it is plainly contrary to the law of nature, however defined, that children should command old men, fools wise men, and that the privileged few should gorge themselves with superfluities, while the starving multitude are in want of the bare necessities of life.

APPENDIX[9]

A FAMOUS author, reckoning up the good and evil of human life, and comparing the aggregates, finds that our pains greatly exceed our pleasures: so that, all things considered, human life is not at all a valuable gift. This conclusion does not surprise me; for the writer drew all his arguments from man in civilisation. Had he gone back to the state of nature, his inquiries would clearly have had a different result, and man would have been seen to be subject to very few evils not of his own creation. It has indeed cost us not a little trouble to make ourselves as wretched as we are. When we consider, on the one hand, the immense labours of mankind, the many sciences brought to perfection, the arts invented, the powers employed, the deeps filled up, the mountains levelled, the rocks shattered, the rivers made navigable, the tracts of land cleared, the lakes emptied, the marshes drained, the enormous structures erected on land, and the teeming vessels that cover the sea; and, on the other hand, estimate with ever so little thought, the real advantages that have accrued from all these works to mankind, we cannot help being amazed at the vast disproportion there is between these things, and deploring the infatuation of man, which, to gratify his silly pride and vain self–admiration, induces him eagerly to pursue all the miseries he is capable of feeling, though beneficent nature had kindly placed them out of his way.

That men are actually wicked, a sad and continual experience of them proves beyond doubt: but, all the same, I think I have shown that man is naturally good. What then can have depraved him to such an extent, except the changes that have happened in his constitution, the advances he has made, and the knowledge he has acquired? We may admire human society as much as we please; it will be none the less true that it necessarily leads men to hate each other in proportion as their interests clash, and to do one another apparent services, while they are really doing every imaginable mischief. What can be thought of a relation, in which the interest of every individual dictates rules directly opposite to those the public reason dictates to the community in general — in which every man finds his profit in the misfortunes of his neighbour? There is not perhaps any man in a comfortable position who has not greedy heirs, and perhaps even children, secretly wishing for his death; not a ship at sea, of which the loss would not be good news to some merchant or other; not a house, which some debtor of bad faith would not be glad to see reduced to ashes with all the papers it contains; not a nation which does not rejoice at the disasters that befall its neighbours. Thus it is that we find our advantage in the misfortunes of our fellow–creatures, and that the loss of one man almost always constitutes the prosperity of another. But it is still more pernicious that public calamities are the objects of the hopes and expectations of innumerable individuals. Some desire sickness, some mortality, some war, and some famine. I have seen men wicked enough to weep for sorrow at the prospect of a plentiful season; and the great and fatal fire of London, which cost so many unhappy persons their lives or their fortunes, made the fortunes of perhaps ten thousand others. I know that Montaigne censures Demades the Athenian for having caused to be punished a workman who, by selling his coffins very dear, was a great gainer by the deaths of his fellow–citizens; but, the reason alleged by Montaigne being that everybody ought to be punished, my point is clearly confirmed by it. Let us penetrate, therefore, the superficial appearances of benevolence, and survey what passes in the inmost recesses of the heart. Let us reflect what must be the state of things, when men are forced to caress and destroy one another at the same time; when they are born enemies by duty, and knaves by interest. It will perhaps be said that society is so formed that every man gains by serving the rest. That would be all very well, if he did not gain still more by injuring them. There is no legitimate profit so great, that it cannot be greatly exceeded by what may be made illegitimately; we always gain more by hurting our neighbours than by doing them good. Nothing is required but to know how to act with impunity; and to this end the powerful employ all their strength, and the weak all their cunning.

Savage man, when he has dined, is at peace with all nature, and the friend of all his fellow–creatures. If a dispute arises about a meal, he rarely comes to blows, without having first compared the difficulty of conquering his antagonist with the trouble of finding subsistence elsewhere: and, as pride does not come in, it all ends in a few blows; the victor eats, and the vanquished seeks provision somewhere else, and all is at peace. The case is quite different with man in the state of society, for whom first necessaries have to be provided, and then superfluities; delicacies follow next, then immense wealth, then subjects, and then slaves. He enjoys not a moment's relaxation; and what is yet stranger, the less natural and pressing his wants, the more headstrong are his passions, and, still worse, the more he has it in his power to gratify them; so that after a long course of prosperity, after having swallowed up treasures and ruined multitudes, the hero ends up by cutting every throat till he finds himself, at last, sole master of the world. Such is in miniature the moral picture, if not of human life, at least of the secret pretensions of the heart of civilised man.

Discourse on Inequality

Compare without partiality the state of the citizen with that of the savage, and trace out, if you can, how many inlets the former has opened to pain and death, besides those of his vices, his wants and his misfortunes. If you reflect on the mental afflictions that prey on us, the violent passions that waste and exhaust us, the excessive labour with which the poor are burdened, the still more dangerous indolence to which the wealthy give themselves up, so that the poor perish of want, and the rich of surfeit; if you reflect but a moment on the heterogeneous mixtures and pernicious seasonings of foods; the corrupt state in which they are frequently eaten; on the adulteration of medicines, the wiles of those who sell them, the mistakes of those who administer them, and the poisonous vessels in which they are prepared; on the epidemics bred by foul air in consequence of great numbers of men being crowded together, or those which are caused by our delicate way of living, by our passing from our houses into the open air and back again, by the putting on or throwing off our clothes with too little care, and by all the precautions which sensuality has converted into necessary habits, and the neglect of which sometimes costs us our life or health; if you take into account the conflagrations and earthquakes, which, devouring or overwhelming whole cities, destroy the inhabitants by thousands; in a word, if you add together all the dangers with which these causes are always threatening us, you will see how dearly nature makes us pay for the contempt with which we have treated her lessons.

I shall not here repeat, what I have elsewhere said of the calamities of war; but wish that those, who have sufficient knowledge, were willing or bold enough to make public the details of the villainies committed in armies by the contractors for commissariat and hospitals: we should see plainly that their monstrous frauds, already none too well concealed, which cripple the finest armies in less than no time, occasion greater destruction among the soldiers than the swords of the enemy.

The number of people who perish annually at sea, by famine, the scurvy, pirates, fire and shipwrecks, affords matter for another shocking calculation. We must also place to the credit of the establishment of property, and consequently to the institution of society, assassinations, poisonings, highway robberies, and even the punishments inflicted on the wretches guilty of these crimes; which, though expedient to prevent greater evils, yet by making the murder of one man cost the lives of two or more, double the loss to the human race.

Discourse on Inequality

What shameful methods are sometimes practised to prevent the birth of men, and cheat nature; either by brutal and depraved appetites which insult her most beautiful work–appetites unknown to savages or mere animals, which can spring only from the corrupt imagination of mankind in civilised countries; or by secret abortions, the fitting effects of debauchery and vitiated notions of honour; or by the exposure or murder of multitudes of infants, who fall victims to the poverty of their parents, or the cruel shame of their mothers; or, finally, by the mutilation of unhappy wretches, part of whose life, with their hope of posterity, is given up to vain singing, or, still worse, the brutal jealousy of other men: a mutilation which, in the last case, becomes a double outrage against nature from the treatment of those who suffer it, and from the use to which they are destined. But is it not a thousand times more common and more dangerous for paternal rights openly to offend against humanity? How many talents have not been thrown away, and inclinations forced, by the unwise constraint of fathers? How many men, who would have distinguished themselves in a fitting estate, have died dishonoured and wretched in another for which they had no taste! How many happy, but unequal, marriages have been broken or disturbed, and how many chaste wives have been dishonoured, by an order of things continually in contradiction with that of nature! How many good and virtuous husbands and wives are reciprocally punished for having been ill–assorted! How many young and unhappy victims of their parents' avarice plunge into vice, or pass their melancholy days in tears, groaning in the indissoluble bonds which their hearts repudiate and gold alone has formed! Fortunate sometimes are those whose courage and virtue remove them from life before inhuman violence makes them spend it in crime or in despair. Forgive me, father and mother, whom I shall ever regret: my complaint embitters your griefs; but would they might be an eternal and terrible example to every one who dares, in the name of nature, to violate her most sacred right.

If I have spoken only of those ill–starred unions which are the result of our system, is it to be thought that those over which love and sympathy preside are free from disadvantages? What if I should undertake to show humanity attacked in its very source, and even in the most sacred of all ties, in which fortune is consulted before nature, and, the disorders of society confounding all virtue and vice, continence becomes a criminal precaution, and a refusal to give life to a fellow–creature, an act of humanity? But, without drawing aside the veil which hides all these horrors, let us content ourselves with pointing out the evil which others will have to remedy.

To all this add the multiplicity of unhealthy trades, which shorten men's lives or destroy their bodies, such as working in the mines, and the preparing of metals and minerals, particularly lead, copper, mercury, cobalt, and arsenic: add those other dangerous trades which are daily fatal to many tilers, carpenters, masons and miners: put all these together and we can see, in the establishment and perfection of societies, the reasons for that diminution of our species, which has been noticed by many philosophers.

Luxury, which cannot be prevented among men who are tenacious of their own convenience and of the respect paid them by others, soon completes the evil society had begun, and, under the pretence of giving bread to the poor, whom it should never have made such, impoverishes all the rest, and sooner or later depopulates the State. Luxury is a remedy much worse than the disease it sets up to cure; or rather it is in itself the greatest of all evils, for every State, great or small: for, in order to maintain all the servants and vagabonds it creates, it brings oppression and ruin on the citizen and the labourer; it is like those scorching winds, which, covering the trees and plants with devouring insects, deprive useful animals of their subsistence and spread famine and death wherever they blow.

From society and the luxury to which it gives birth arise the liberal and mechanical arts, commerce, letters, and all those superfluities which make industry flourish, and enrich and ruin nations. The reason for such destruction is plain. It is easy to see, from the very nature of agriculture, that it must be the least lucrative of all the arts; for, its produce being the most universally necessary, the price must be proportionate to the abilities of the very poorest of mankind.

From the same principle may be deduced this rule, that the arts in general are more lucrative in proportion as they are less useful; and that, in the end, the most useful becomes the most neglected. From this we may learn what to think of the real advantages of industry and the actual effects of its progress.

Such are the sensible causes of all the miseries, into which opulence at length plunges the most celebrated nations. In proportion as arts and industry flourish, the despised husbandman, burdened with the taxes necessary for the support of luxury, and condemned to pass his days between labour and hunger, forsakes his native field, to seek in towns the bread he ought to carry thither. The more our capital cities strike the vulgar eye with admiration, the greater reason is there to lament the sight of the abandoned countryside, the large tracts of land that lie uncultivated, the roads crowded with unfortunate citizens turned beggars or highwaymen, and doomed to end their wretched lives either on a dunghill or on the gallows. Thus the State grows rich on the one hand, and feeble and depopulated on the other; the mightiest monarchies, after having taken immense pains to enrich and depopulate themselves, fall at last a prey to some poor nation, which has yielded to the fatal temptation of invading them, and then, growing opulent and weak in its turn, is itself invaded and ruined by some other.

Let any one inform us what produced the swarms of barbarians, who overran Europe, Asia and Africa for so many ages. Was their prodigious increase due to their industry and arts, to the wisdom of their laws, or to the excellence of their political system? Let the learned tell us why, instead of multiplying to such a degree, these fierce and brutal men, without sense or science, without education, without restraint, did not destroy each other hourly in quarrelling over the productions of their fields and woods. Let them tell us how these wretches could have the presumption to oppose such clever people as we were, so well trained in military discipline, and possessed of such excellent laws and institutions: and why, since society has been brought to perfection in northern countries, and so much pains taken to instruct their inhabitants in their social duties and in the art of living happily and peaceably together, we see them no longer produce such numberless hosts as they used once to send forth to be the plague and terror of other nations. I fear some one may at last answer me by saying, that all these fine things, arts, sciences and laws, were wisely invented by men, as a salutary plague, to prevent the too great multiplication of mankind, lest the world, which was given us for a habitation, should in time be too small for its inhabitants.

What, then, is to be done? Must societies be totally abolished? Must meum and tuum be annihilated, and must we return again to the forests to live among bears? This is a deduction in the manner of my adversaries, which I would as soon anticipate as let them have the shame of drawing. O you, who have never heard the voice of heaven, who think man destined only to live this little life and die in peace; you, who can resign in the midst of populous cities your fatal acquisitions, your restless spirits, your corrupt hearts and endless desires; resume, since it depends entirely on ourselves, your ancient and primitive innocence: retire to the woods, there to lose the sight and remembrance of the crimes of your contemporaries; and be not apprehensive of degrading your species, by renouncing its advances in order to renounce its vices. As for men like me, whose passions have destroyed their original simplicity, who can no longer subsist on plants or acorns, or live without laws and magistrates; those who were honoured in their first father with supernatural instructions; those who discover, in the design of giving human actions at the start a morality which they must otherwise have been so long in acquiring, the reason for a precept in itself indifferent and inexplicable on every other system; those, in short, who are persuaded that the Divine Being has called all mankind to be partakers in the happiness and perfection of celestial intelligences, all these will endeavour to merit the eternal prize they are to expect from the practice of those virtues, which they make themselves follow in learning to know them. They will respect the sacred bonds of their respective communities; they will love their fellow–citizens, and serve them with all their might: they will scrupulously obey the laws, and all those who make or administer them; they will particularly honour those wise and good princes, who find means of preventing, curing or even palliating all these evils and abuses, by which we are constantly threatened; they will animate the zeal of their deserving rulers, by showing them, without flattery or fear, the importance of their office and the severity of their duty. But they will not therefore have less contempt for a constitution that cannot support itself without the aid of so many splendid characters, much oftener wished for than found; and from which, notwithstanding all their pains and solicitude, there always arise more real calamities than even apparent advantages.

---

1. See Appendix.

2. Justin, Hist. ii. 2. So much more does the ignorance of vice profit the one sort than the knowledge of virtue the other.

3. Egoism must not be confused with self–respect: for they differ both in themselves and in their effects. Self–respect is a natural feeling which leads every animal to look to its own preservation, and which, guided in man by reason and modified by compassion, creates humanity and virtue. Egoism is a purely relative and factitious feeling, which arises in the state of society, leads each individual to make more of himself than of any other, causes all the mutual damage men inflict one on another, and is the real source of the "sense of honour." This being understood, I maintain that, in our primitive condition, in the true state of nature, egoism did not exist; for as each man regarded himself as the only observer of his actions, the only being in the universe who took any interest in him, and the sole judge of his deserts, no feeling arising from comparisons he could not be led

to make could take root in his soul; and for the same reason, he could know neither hatred nor the desire for revenge, since these passions can spring only from a sense of injury: and as it is the contempt or the intention to hurt, and not the harm done, which constitutes the injury, men who neither valued nor compared themselves could do one another much violence, when it suited them, without feeling any sense of injury. In a word, each man, regarding his fellows almost as he regarded animals of different species, might seize the prey of a weaker or yield up his own to a stronger, and yet consider these acts of violence as mere natural occurrences, without the slightest emotion of insolence or despite, or any other feeling than the joy or grief of success or failure.

4. Nature avows she gave the human race the softest hearts, who gave them tears.

5. Ovid, Metamorphoses, xi. 127.

Both rich and poor, shocked at their new—found ills, Would fly from wealth, and lose what they had sought.

6. Tacitus, Hist. iv. 17. The most wretched slavery they call peace.

7. Of the Rights of the Most Christian Queen over Various States of the Monarchy of Spain, 1667.

8. Distributive justice would oppose this rigorous equality of the state of nature, even were it practicable in civil society; as all the members of the State owe it their services in proportion to their talents and abilities, they ought, on their side, to be distinguished and favoured in proportion to the services they have actually rendered. It is in this sense we must understand that passage of Isocrates, in which he extols the primitive Athenians, for having determined which of the two kinds of equality was the most useful, viz., that which consists in dividing the same advantages indiscriminately among all the citizens, or that which consists in distributing them to each according to his deserts. These able politicians, adds the orator, banishing that unjust inequality which makes no distinction between good and bad men, adhered inviolably to that which rewards and punishes every man according to his deserts.

But in the first place, there never existed a society, however corrupt some may have become, where no difference was made between the good and the bad; and with regard to

73

morality, where no measures can be prescribed by law exact enough to serve as a practical rule for a magistrate, it is with great prudence that, in order not to leave the fortune or quality of the citizens to his discretion, it prohibits him from passing judgment on persons and confines his judgment to actions. Only morals such as those of the ancient Romans can bear censors, and such a tribunal among us would throw everything into confusion. The difference between good and bad men is determined by public esteem; the magistrate being strictly a judge of right alone; whereas the public is the truest judge of morals, and is of such integrity and penetration on this head, that although it may be sometimes deceived, it can never be corrupted. The rank of citizens ought, therefore, to be regulated, not according to their personal merit — for this would put it in the power of the magistrate to apply the law almost arbitrarily — but according to the actual services done to the State, which are capable of being more exactly estimated.

9. Part I, para. 17.

CPSIA information can be obtained at www.ICGtesting.com
Printed in the USA
LVOW051436291112

309386LV00010B/241/P